Stop Doing, Start Leading

How to Shift from Doing the Work Yourself
to Becoming a Great Leader

Sue Coyne

www.suecoyne.com

Leadership
Stop Doing, Start Leading
How to Shift from Doing the Work Yourself
to Becoming a Great Leader

Published by
10-10-10 Publishing
Markham, ON
CANADA

British Library Cataloguing in Publication Data.
A catalogue record for this book is available from the British Library.

Contents

Foreword   xi

Prelude   xv

Chapter 1: The Bigger Picture   1

Chapter 2: The Six Keys to Stop Doing and Start Leading   9

Chapter 3: Building Brand You   21

Chapter 4: Growing Your Confidence   45

Chapter 5: The Zero Burnout Strategy   67

Chapter 6: Creating the Time and Energy to Lead   73

Chapter 7: Being a Healthy Leader   85

Chapter 8: Being a Happy Leader   103

Chapter 9: Empowering Yourself and Others   117

Chapter 10: Developing the Potential of Your People   145

Chapter 11: Engaging the People who Influence your Results   177

Chapter 12: Your Future – Stop Doing, Start Leading Today   211

Notes   218

Resources   220

Gratitude   225

I dedicate this book to Alex and Millie Coyne, my two children (now adults). They are a constant source of love, learning and support.

Praise for Stop Doing, Start Leading

"If you aspire to be a great leader, this book is for you. It addresses the core issue of leadership: inspiring and engaging your employees to bring their full selves to work. Based on years of accumulated wisdom Sue describes what you must do to get the best out of your people."

Richard Barrett, Founder and Chairman of the Barrett Values Centre, www.richardbarrett.net

"A great book for the business owner shifting from expert to an inspiring leader."

Andy Harrington
Sunday Times Best Selling Author of Passion Into Profit

"Sue writes as she is: warm, clear and complete. I have read many management and leadership books but none have given me such a complete guide to personal leadership as Stop Doing, Start Leading. I particularly like the focus on behavior, mindset and insight as the keys to developing an Authentic Leadership Brand. I experienced this in my sessions with Sue and it has made a big impact on me."

Gerard de Reuver, former client and President of DSM Dyneema

"In Stop Doing, Start Leading, Sue Coyne guides us on the personal journey from 'being the expert' to a place where we can truly lead others, helping them develop their own talents. Coyne draws on her own experience as a manager and mother, and illustrates her points with engaging stories from her coaching practice. She shows us how to step out of the 'expert syndrome' by clarifying our own unique, authentic approach to leadership. Coyne helps us see how our inner state impacts our leadership capacity, then shows us how to shift out of burnout and gain the confidence, balance and, yes, the inner happiness we need to stay resilient and effectively lead others. She goes on to reveal how we can grow as leaders by engaging, empowering and developing others. I recommend this book to anyone who wants to take their next step in growing as a person and as a leader."

Bill Joiner, co-author, Leadership Agility

"Sue's book draws on her own personal experience of leadership and its challenges as a leader in her own right, and as an insightful and effective coach. It provides important advice for anyone contemplating or indeed currently in a leadership role. The chapters on personal energy management and taking responsibility for your own wellbeing are particularly valuable and illustrate perfectly Sue's human approach to the topic of leadership."

Janet Soo-Chung CBE, former client and CEO of North Lancashire PCT

"Sue's book is an intelligent, thought-through, warm-hearted and profoundly practical book for those who really want to make a difference, not solely in terms of business results but also for the people they lead."

Myles Downey, author of Effective Modern Coaching and Enabling Genius - A Mindset for Success in the 21st Century,

www.mylesdowney.com

"In a world where stakeholders are increasingly focused on what a company stands for as much as what it does, this is a leadership book very much for its time. It is full of insight that will help you develop your own authentic leadership style."

Chris Oglesby, former client, CEO of Bruntwood,

www.bruntwood.co.uk

"This book is a great guide to the people and relationship side of leadership. Sue makes it very accessible and clear so as a leader I can readily relate to the ideas, concepts and approaches. There is the invitation to reflect on the learning and insights she provides and try them out in practice so she engages you in the challenges of being a leader. This book is great if you are stepping up into a leadership position and guides you to the style of leadership that is authentic for you. If you take this seriously you will undoubtedly shift from doing to leading."

John Leary-Joyce, President of the Academy of Executive Coaching,

www.aoec.com

"As the pace of change continues to accelerate, the need for leaders to create an environment of trust in which individuals and their organizations thrive, becomes even more important. Sue's book challenges current and aspiring leaders to reflect on how they are being (in addition to what they are doing) by drawing on a wide range of perspectives. A valuable read - enjoy the journey!"

Sue Swanborough, HR Director, General Mills Northern Europe

Foreword

It is a pleasure to welcome this book by Sue Coyne, which is timely, apposite and practical. I read it while in the middle of leading global research on "Developing Tomorrow's Leadership Today", led out of Henley Business School and involving research partners around the world. We have interviewed CEOs, HR Directors and Millennial Leaders of Tomorrow from 50 leading companies across sectors and countries, as well as reviewing the top global surveys of CEOs, H.R. Directors and Millennials. Many of the emerging themes and challenges are echoed in this very practical and informative book by Sue Coyne.

Many CEOs talked about the impact of accelerating digitalization. Some quoted the recent research that indicates that nearly half of the current jobs in the USA will no longer exist in twenty years. Some spoke of "the hollowing out of organizations", where many of the jobs in the middle of the organization were being done by computers. Even for jobs that were just a few years ago seen as safe, such as in medicine, law or professional services, we are now creating programs that can perform better than humans.

Some CEOs commented on how knowledge and expertise is becoming less and less a competitive advantage and the only sustainable competitive advantages are the ability to learn faster than your competitors and in how easy you are to do business with.

Not surprisingly, this is echoed by H.R. Directors and heads of Leadership Development when describing what young leaders need to do to progress. "Intellectual curiosity" and "Learning agility" are becoming the leading attributes employers are looking at when hiring and promoting someone. They also emphasize the growing demand for managers and leaders to be able to engage, motivate and partner with people across age groups, cultures, functions, sectors and a wide range of stakeholders.

One H.R. Director talked of the four steps in leadership:

1. Doing the work yourself, and perhaps managing a few others who do the same work
2. Adding value through leading and enabling a team of others to do the work
3. Leading a larger cohort of people who you know and whose work you know, but many only virtually, indirectly or intermittently
4. Leading a business of people from different functions, geographies, disciplines etc. – where your job is to lead and develop the leaders

This parallels the stages of vertical leadership development that have been written about by such writers as Bill Torbert and Bill Joiner, as well as in my own model of the developmental stages of leadership of teams (Hawkins, 2014). In this model I illustrate how many leaders move through the following stages:

1. **Team Manager:** who runs around managing all the individual team members and setting individual targets and following up on performance. Often their engagement style starts with "You should – you must..." This is similar to Bill Joiner and Bill Tolbert's "Expert -Technician leader".

2. **Team Leader:** who steps back and focuses on the collective goals the team must achieve. Often their engagement style starts with "We need to focus on – we need to achieve..." This is similar to Bill Joiner and Bill Torbert's "Achiever leader".

3. **Team Orchestrator:** who focuses on enabling the connections both within the team and between the team and its critical stakeholders. Often their engagement style starts with "Who do you need to connect with to take that forward?" This is similar to Bill Joiner's "Catalyst Leader" and Bill Torbert's "Individualist Leader".

4. **Team Coach:** who focuses on developing the collective capacity of the team and its members in line with the needs of its changing stakeholder eco-system. Often their engagement style starts with "Who do we serve? What will they need from us that is different in the future? How do we develop that capacity?" This is similar to Bill Joiner's "Co-creator and Synergist leaders", and Bill Torbert's "Strategist Leader".

But we must remember that although maps can help us see the wider terrain and map our journey, the map is not the territory. I have had the honor and pleasure of watching Sue Coyne make this journey in her own work and what Sue does brilliantly in this book is show the useful stepping stones in moving from a person who manages by being the one who knows, to leading by enabling others. Sooner rather than later this is a journey everyone will need to go on. Take this book with you in your rucksack.

Peter Hawkins, Professor of Leadership, Henley Business School, Chairman Renewal Associates, www.renewalasociates.co.uk, May 2016.

Frey, C.B. & Osborne, M.A. (2013) *THE FUTURE OF EMPLOYMENT: HOW SUSCEPTIBLE ARE JOBS TO COMPUTERISATION?* www.oxfordmartin.ox.ac.uk/downloads/academic/The_Future_of_Employment.pdf(Accessed May 1st 2016).

Hawkins, P. (2011, 2014) *Leadership Team Coaching: Developing Collective Transformational Leadership* London: Kogan Page

Joiner, B. & Josephs S. (2006) *Leadership Agility: Five Levels of Mastery for Anticipating and Initiating Change* San Francisco: Jossey-Bass/Wiley

Torbert, W.R. & Rooke, D,. (2005) 7 Transformations of Leadership. *Harvard Business Review* 2005; 83(4): 67-76.

Prelude

1. The Wake-Up Call

It's 5 o'clock on a pitch black April morning back in 2000. My suitcase is in the hallway and there's a taxi waiting outside.

Briefcase in hand, crisp Armani suit, ready to go, I'm standing in my children's bedroom between their twin beds and I can just make out a little golden head on the pillow of each bed. I quietly whisper to each of them, "Bye my precious. Mummy will be back very soon."

I feel torn. The head chatter starts. I'm guessing you get that too...

"Why am I doing this? What kind of a mother am I? How are they going to feel when they realize that I will be away from them for another three nights? I'm an outsider in their lives. I don't even know any of the people at their school."

I can hear the other voice inside my head answering my question in a strident, bossy tone:

"You're speaking at the Brighton Conference Centre, that's why you're doing this. So you can share your ideas with **all** of those people, to position yourself and the company as **thought** leaders. You know it's going to be worth the sacrifice. And as you often say, you are doing it for the children so they can have a good education and a great lifestyle."

I push my shoulders back into my suit jacket and reply to myself, "Yes it's about being significant and important and the lifestyle – that's why I'm doing it."

Let me ask you this. Have you ever made choices based on creating happiness for the future? What impact have those choices had on your life? Do you think that happiness is something that should be postponed?

I had often heard people say that tomorrow may never come, so be happy today. That very message was about to be brought home to me and I just didn't see it coming.

Some mistakes are more expensive than others

Fast forward three months to July. I'm in hospital, in a cancer ward. I'm in an isolation room. The nurses are wearing white plastic aprons and face masks so I can only see their eyes but I can sense their concern.

That day in April when I gave that speech at the Brighton Conference Centre was the day that I discovered I had cancer. The same day I left my children behind tucked up in their beds.

We all get voices in our heads. Does yours give you a hard time too?

On this occasion my inner voice was sounding unusually reflective:

"I can't help noticing the irony in this situation. My oncologist, poor devil, has probably been working 20 hours a day and squeezing in private work to send his children to private school. No wonder he's made a mistake. Ironic because that's how my life is. I wonder how many mistakes I have made through working ridiculously long hours."

My children are there but they can't even come in to see me. They can just peep through the glass window. It was pretty scary for them and for me. I really did think in that moment I was going to die. Not of the cancer but of an accidentally dispensed chemotherapy overdose.

This really brought home to me that you never know what life is going to throw at you.

Events like this can be an opportunity as they make you see things from a different perspective. You start to ask yourself important questions, such as:

What if my life is to end here in this hospital bed?

What would I miss?
What would people remember me for?
Would they know what I stand for?
Do I know myself what I stand for?

Have you ever asked yourself those sorts of questions?

In that hospital room I had a sudden and powerful realization that something had to change. My life was crazily out of balance. I was not only jeopardizing my own life, I was playing Russian roulette with the happiness of my children and the future that I wanted to create for them and *with* them. I determined that day that I wanted to live to see my grandchildren and that if that were to be the case I needed to completely change my definition of success.

Do you listen to your body when it lets you know you are doing too much?

Unfortunately, I didn't. I worked through many colds and often fell asleep at the dinner table. I was so focused on the success of the business that my body didn't get a look in. I needed a wake-up call to get me to see what I was doing. I was very lucky. I came through the chemotherapy overdose. I was also lucky that we sold the business as planned shortly afterwards and I chose not to stay on. As a result, I was able to leave with a bit of money that gave me some breathing space.

Another casualty of my over-focusing on work was my marriage. Divorce followed shortly after we sold the business. I invested in coaching training, initially to help me through the after effects of the cancer, my business burnout and the divorce.

That was the start of my coaching career. I determined that I would use it to help myself to live a more balanced life and find a different definition of success. I also wanted to enable the leaders who I worked with to do the same without having to have the same sort of wake-up call that I had.

What I didn't understand then that I do now is that when our definition of success is linked to working harder (and overworking as a result), and believing that hard work is the route to high performance and exceptional results, we have a flawed model for being successful.

Success is not about striving and surviving. It's about thriving.

Now you can understand why it matters so much to me that leaders are not only great at what they do, but that they are sustainably effective while they do it.

It's why I had to write this book. I hope it will help you to discover for yourself why it's so important to *Stop Doing and Start Leading*. You are capable of becoming a great leader without sacrificing your life or family in the process, and this book will help you do it.

2. The Ripple Effect

It's October 2011, and I'm enjoying dinner in the restaurant of a beautiful chateau in France. It is an elegant restaurant with high ceilings and attentive waiters dressed all in black with crisp white aprons. There aren't many people in the restaurant and we have a round table at the back of the room.

I say we. I am sitting with eight leaders. I look around the table at the faces I have grown so fond of. There is a feisty Belgian woman, a Divisional Director; a Dutch woman in charge of innovation who had recently joined the team and brought a bit more balance; a Scottish HR Director and English Strategy Director who are full of friendly banter; a suave German man, another Divisional Director; and four French guys: a people-oriented FD; a tall, balding, inspirational President; a bespectacled Operations Director with a thoughtful side; and another Divisional Director who is tall, dark and decisive.

Apart from the HR Director and FD, they all have an engineering or scientific background and so tend to be quite logical and left-brained.

When I started working with this team four years earlier they didn't know how to spell emotion, and they certainly didn't regard it as part of being intelligent! They really struggled when I encouraged them to end each of our team coaching sessions with a round of appreciation.

So, you can imagine how surprised I was when the Belgian woman stood up with a small book in her hand, which said on the front, "A Round of Appreciation for Sue."

One by one, they stood up, read what they had written in the book and passed it on:

"I admire your journey, the way you have become a new person, quitting your job, starting a new profession – INSPIRATIONAL."

"You got us all out of our comfort zones. You achieved with us a great big step in openness."

"You helped me reach the stars, the moon, the milky-way and beyond."

"I felt the immediate click, your willingness to experiment, perseverance through all the challenges..."

"Tight-rope walker – it appears easy but it requires preparation! Balance-directive and open. A transformation for the whole team!"

"You put everything into perspective and brought me to a better balance!"

"You helped me get to where I am today and what you have done for the whole organization is fabulous."

"Thank you for getting us out of our comfort zones. Thank goodness our direct reports couldn't see us! We started 100 percent rational a couple of years back. Your coaching got us to 100 percent emotion!" "Result orientation was fine but inspirational leadership was outstanding."

Tears running down my face, I forced each of them to accept a huge hug. I thanked them for the privilege of working with them and witnessing them grow into such an amazing team.

Looking back at the events that led to this, the difficult journey that has now brought these rich rewards, I know in my heart that I made the right decision back in 2002 when we sold the business.

The ripple effect that is happening as a result of the willingness of these eight leaders to get out of their comfort zones and grow, not only as leaders but as human beings, will make a difference through all of the people that they touch. Their business colleagues, their families and their teams will all have better lives. It's truly incredible to see what happens when you Stop Doing and Start Leading.

Now it's your turn.

3. Your Journey to Becoming a Great Leader

Even great leaders like Sir Alex Ferguson, who led Manchester United Football Club for 26 successful years, had to find out how to stop doing and start leading.

"I never had any formal schooling to be a leader... In my younger years I automatically assumed that if I did something myself it was the quickest and best way to get anything done. Nobody had ever explained to me that working with and through others is by far the most effective way to do things, assuming of course that they understand what you want and are keen to follow... I had never managed a team and didn't understand how working through people allowed you to do more and amplified your reach... I gradually came to understand the difference between management and leadership and that my job (as a leader) was to set very high standards, to help everyone believe they could do things they didn't think they were capable of, to chart a course that hadn't been pursued before and make everyone understand that the impossible was possible." [1]

Maybe you are reading this book because you are already great at what you *do* but, like Sir Alex, you are not sure what it takes to *be* a great leader. As a result, perhaps you are focusing on *doing* everything yourself. Doing what you know how to do feels comfortable doesn't it? It probably also means you are working long hours and carrying a lot of unnecessary stress.

There may also be a part of you that is curious and even excited at the possibility of growing into *being* a great leader, but you are not sure where to start. Leadership skills can be learnt, they also improve with practice. Most of what you need to be a great leader though comes from within and is already there waiting to be allowed out to see the light of day.

If, like Sir Alex, you find yourself in a leadership role without the support and training you need to cope, develop and thrive as a leader, you're in the right place.

This book has been written to help you do exactly that, whether you are a leader in the making, a manager who has been promoted to a leadership position or an expert thrown in at the deep end, *Stop Doing Start Leading* will help you to understand why we can all get into hot water when we need to let go, delegate, inspire and lead others.

It will help you find your path to becoming a great leader. Without a clear path you could find yourself washed-up, burned-out and very unhappy. Would you like to work with yourself when you are like that?

No. And nor will anyone else.

It's not just about getting the job done. It's about getting it done in a sustainable way so that you and the business can grow as people pull together for the cause.

How YOU are going to get there

I'm confident that the time you invest in this book will be more than repaid by your growth as a leader, your ability to get results through people and your impact on the success of your organization through delivering sustainable high performances. Imagine how it will feel to be less stressed and overwhelmed and to have more time to enjoy your life outside of work.

With this book, my aim is to help you to discover *what* it means to be a great leader and *why* it matters to you. I will also share with you *how* you can lead in a way that is sustainable for you and your people. If Sir Alex can have 26 years of successful leadership why can't you? If you want to go into more detail on *how* to lead, my online program The Effective Leadership Launcher has even more detail on how to develop your abilities in each aspect of leadership covered in this book. You can find out more information about this program here: **www.suecoyneleadershipacademy.com**

Besides what you can learn in this book, I have created some valuable bonuses for you. To help you identify your priorities and focus on what makes you a great leader, there is an e-book on Creating the Time to

Lead. If you want to find out who you are as a leader there is a workbook on Creating Your Authentic Leadership Brand. To support you in effectively empowering your people there is a bonus chapter on the Core Capabilities of Empowerment which include building trust and rapport, developing your emotional intelligence and being able to adapt your leadership style. In addition, there is a bonus chapter on Catalyzing Change in Yourself and Others, an essential skill for leading in the 21st century. Finally, there is a PDF on How to Re-wire Limiting Beliefs. You can access all of these bonuses by going to **https://suecoyne.com/stopdoingstartleading/**

In this book, I share with you the latest leadership thinking, neuroscience and stories based on working with leaders since 2003. I am going to share with you the same strategies that helped them to stop struggling and start thriving. At the end of each chapter I have created a space for you to reflect on where you are in relation to what you have learnt and why it matters to you to grow in this aspect of leadership. It is then up to you to determine how this is relevant to you and how you are going to experiment with it in your day-to-day leadership role.

I know that you have it within you to be a great leader and I hope that this book is a source of inspiration for you.

Enjoy the growth opportunity you are giving yourself through this book.

Chapter 1
The Bigger Picture

"The most exciting breakthroughs of the twenty-first century will not occur because of technology, but because of an expanding concept of what it means to be human." - John Naisbitt

An unlikely messenger

Have you ever been to an event where you have listened to speech after speech and not really learnt anything new and you have been sitting for so long that your bottom is numb? I think anyone in business has been to one of those conferences.

I'm in one. There's no natural light in this basement conference room. The chairs are a bit too close together and your thighs are almost touching the person in the next chair. Awkward. Long rows of chairs make it difficult to get up without creating a disturbance and you are stuck in the middle. It is one of those days and the questions are whizzing round my head as I am twitching to leave. "What will he know about this subject? I wonder if I can leave early and at least get home at a reasonable time?" I move to the end of the row nearest to the door as a first step.

But it's too late.

He walks onto the stage with his Einstein-like white hair, open collar, brown pinstriped suit and sunglasses! Seriously? He was probably the most disheveled looking person in the whole conference room. A total contrast in appearance and language to the previous corporate speakers. He went for the shock tactics and there was no way I was going home. I couldn't take my eyes off this guy.

Pacing the stage with agitation he says something that really hits home:

"100 years later we are back where we were, a new world struggling with an old structure that is no longer fit for purpose. If businesses want to be successful they need to be authentic, genuine and real".

Did what he say resonate with the room? You bet it did! It certainly resonated with me. I could have written his script for him. Sir Bob Geldof not only spoke passionately about the need for a new approach to business more attuned to the 21st century and one centered around trust, but his whole demeanor smashed the out-dated 20th century paradigm that he was rallying against.

The old power paradigm – it's time to shift

The 20th century view of the world that Sir Bob was fuming about is one you are probably very familiar with. It's a view that sees organizations as machines and people as cogs inside them. Maybe you've been a machine creator or maybe you've been a cog.

A characteristic of the 20th century mindset is that power is held by the few. "It is jealously guarded... closed, inaccessible and leader-driven." This view of the world has created a breed of leaders who use command and control to get things done, who often believe that they are all-powerful, know best and deserve special treatment and perks. We used to look up to these superhero leaders but times have changed. As a result of numerous scandals and crises including the financial crisis in the West created by the bankers in 2008 and Volkswagen falsifying emission tests in 2015, plus many more shameful examples, **trust in business leaders is at a low ebb.**

What do you believe is the cause of all of this?

Could it be that the **relentless focus** in many businesses **on short-term financial results** and keeping their shareholders happy causes (or even forces) their leaders to do whatever it takes to meet their objectives?

So, why is it these superhero leaders so easily fall into command and control?

The answer is simple: often they don't actually **know how** to get people to do things any other way.

What do they get out of leading in this way? When people do what they tell them to do and look to them for all the answers it's understandable that it gives them a feeling of significance.

So why does this matter? It can be really stressful for leaders to feel they have to know everything and be in control of everything. It's heart attack material for the leader, and the negative impact it has on other people makes it totally unsustainable in the longer term. When leaders behave in this way it leads to people feeling mistrusted and resentful. Trust erodes, confidence declines, efficiencies erode and business suffers. People are left as casualties by the side of the road.

Stressed out or blissed out – which one are you?

Let me introduce you to a classic, old-style command and control leader. Ronnie is CEO at Best Computers Ltd. You know the type: red tie, braces and smart designer suit. It's the quarter end coming up on Friday and his mind is in overdrive. He hasn't slept a wink all night. He strides into the office without acknowledging anyone and heads for the sales department. The signs of stress are visible on the faces of the sales team. They absorb the pressure from Ronnie as he barks orders at them to get the last deals closed. They have that worn down and worn out look. It's always like this every quarter, year in year out.

He's relentless.

Maybe you're like Ronnie and are feeling the stress. Or perhaps you've been on the receiving end of this type of leadership.

It doesn't have to be like that. Meet Eric, CEO of Partners in Success. His day is shaping up very differently. He's the relaxed guy in chinos and an open collared shirt.

He believes in management by walking about. He stops to have a chat with Ann, the receptionist, as he walks into the office. He has just taken Gemma, his 10-year-old daughter, to school and is looking forward to attending her school concert with his wife later in the week. His team has compiled a report on the key business indicators for him. The one that interests him more than anything is employee engagement; Eric knows that it's his best predictor of the future financial performance of the business. He's delighted to see that it has reached a new high and calls in each member of his team personally to congratulate them. Eric knows that happy, engaged leaders create an environment in which people enjoy their work and are in turn engaged, self-motivated and productive. He loves his job!

So, what is the difference? Why are leaders like Ronnie always running around stressing not just themselves but everyone else as well? People like Ronnie dread Monday mornings. Eric, on the other hand, can't wait to get out of bed and get into work.

Which one are you?

It doesn't matter where you are starting from

Are you treating people as cogs in the machine or as human beings? Your answer to this may depend on your situation, the context of where you work and your background.

Many of the leaders I have worked with over the years spent much of their careers becoming an expert; for example, they were trained to be a finance specialist, a lawyer, a scientist, an engineer, an IT specialist etc. and as a result they were valued for their knowledge and expertise. When the time came and they found themselves promoted to a leadership position, all of a sudden they felt unsure of themselves. They didn't feel they were experts in leadership and not being *the* expert in their situation was daunting new territory. It took them out of their comfort zone.

Possibly this is something you could have experienced yourself. It's not a great place to be!

Or, maybe you're not formally in a management or leadership position, but you want to show leadership and make a difference. I believe that this type of informal leadership that's distributed subtly through the veins of an organization is what's required in the 21st century. I refer to it as being *leaderful*.

Or maybe you recognized Ronnie earlier in this chapter and were horrified to realize your style is command and control and sense that it's not appropriate anymore and want to change. You sense the difference needed for a 21st century organization and want to stay relevant and continue to contribute to the success of your organization. If you recognized Ronnie and want to change your leadership style to one that's more sustainable for you (and everyone else), then you will find the answers as you read on.

It's up to you to create the conditions

Organizations are made up of people, and people are living beings, not parts of a machine. That is what we need to recognize in the 21st century. This means your role as a leader is to create the conditions in which people can thrive. This starts with you stopping yourself from doing the tasks that your people should be doing, and instead starting to focus on creating the conditions where you can thrive so that you are in a position to help everyone else thrive. So, are you ready to Stop Doing and Start Leading?

Chapter 2
The Six Keys to Stop Doing and Start Leading

"There is no passion to be found in playing small, in settling for a life that is less than the one you are capable of living." - Nelson Mandela

When I was making the transition from being a market research consultant to a divisional leader and Board Director I spent a lot of time reading books on leadership and attending courses. It was a slow process and meant I worked even longer hours that had a detrimental effect on my health and family life. As you have already heard, cancer/burnout and divorce followed.

Since becoming a leadership coach in 2003 I have trained, mentored and coached many leaders in your situation. I have kept detailed records of what works best, hasn't worked so well and what the biggest commonalities are. *Stop Doing, Start Leading* has been written partly as a result of the wealth of experience inside those records. When I stepped back to take a wider view of this information I saw patterns that were irrefutable.

The first thing I noticed was that most struggling leaders focus almost entirely on *what* they do; they are task focused. There is very little attention on *why* they are doing what they do, and even less on *how* they lead.

As I reviewed my notes I reflected that the *how* of leadership has changed so much since I first became a leader in the 1990s. Since then, science has given us a window into how our brains work. We can actually see how our neurons fire, how our emotions affect our biology and neurology. MRI and other techniques and research have transformed our understanding of how we tick.

The old command and control style of leadership has been shown by neuroscience to be ineffective. We understand better than ever how power and control used bluntly change our brain chemistry and make us less effective. And the context in which we as leaders operate has changed beyond recognition in recent years. The pace of change is relentless, the business world is ever more complex and leaders are dealing with huge amounts of information thrown at them 24/7; and just to complicate things, Generations X (born 1965 – 1984) and Y (born 1984 to 2000) now *expect* engagement and fulfillment at work. Generation Y, or Millennials as they are often called, are different so we have to keep up with how to lead the different generations so our organizations can thrive in the future.

It's hardly surprising that you are time poor and probably find it difficult to create the space to keep up to date and stay relevant as a leader. But don't worry!

Over the years of helping leaders (even struggling leaders!) to become great leaders and do that in a sustainable way, it's become clear that there are **six key areas** that consistently help with all the challenges we have talked about. These aren't related to the *what* of leadership but to the *why* and *how*. If that sounds a little strange, read on. You are about to discover the six key areas that can help you to *Stop Doing and Start Leading*.

The six key areas are:
- Identity
- Balance
- Empowerment
- Development
- Engagement
- Change

So, let's take a quick tour around what those words really mean for you as a leader and how you can put them to work for you.

Identity

Let me ask you something. Is your identity based on the technical expertise that you have built up over the years or on being a great leader? This is the quandary that puts most leaders into that no-man's land of not knowing *who* they truly are in their leadership role. A symptom of not knowing who you are as a leader is that you feel on shaky ground with regard to leadership, and are uncomfortable with your lack of expertise. After all, you got to be a leader in the first place because you *were* an expert. It's a catch-22.

Ask yourself whether it is possible to be a great leader if you aren't sure of your identity as a leader.

I believe that to become a great leader you need to know who you are as a leader and the difference you want to make through your leadership.

Let's shine a light on why this is the case. Having a clear sense of identity means that you know your *why* as a leader, which means that you are more likely to win the hearts *and* the minds of your people, which will give you more influence and a greater ability to inspire and motivate them to give their best.

We will be exploring your sense of leadership identity in a later chapter.

Balance

One of the patterns that was clear from my work with leaders was that many of them struggle to get balance in their lives. Maybe that applies to you too. The symptoms include working long hours and not having enough time to spend with your friends and family, not feeling happy and not having enough enjoyment in your life. Not having the time to look after yourself so you can stay healthy and not having the energy to continue to be successful at work *and* do all the things you want to do in your life. You might even worry that if it carries on like this you will burn out.

Is this desire for more balance something that resonates with you?

Empowerment

So once you have got these two foundational areas sorted out the next most important thing is to know how to step up and be a leader. Let me explain what I mean.

For you to step up as a leader you need to be able to delegate to and empower others. To do that what you need is trust; trust in yourself that you can be an effective leader and trust in others that they can deliver so that you don't have to do everything yourself. Trust allows you to Stop Doing and Start Leading. It's too easy to find yourself involved in the detail, doing things yourself and not empowering people. The result is that you get frustrated and dissatisfied with your performance and so do the people around you.

Development

The fourth key thing I have learnt is that when empowerment and trust are low, task-focused leaders often spend very little time on developing their people.

One of the reasons why this lack of trust happens is that many people, especially those who are experts in their field, get their motivation from delivering results through their own efforts. However, as a leader, you have to continue to learn and grow and for that to be possible *your people* have to learn and grow. As a leader, this becomes your responsibility. When you learn the skills to develop people, create the time and space to grow and develop yourself it has a compound effect on you, your team and the business.

Can you see why continuous learning and growth are key to becoming a great leader?

Engagement

Your employees/team are only one of your stakeholders, albeit a key one. As a leader, you have several stakeholders and you need to engage them all to deliver positive outcomes. Engagement is the fifth key required to become a great leader.

Many of the leaders I work with do not yet know how to take the time to stand back and map out these stakeholders. They haven't been given the skills to develop a stakeholder engagement strategy so they can clarify who they need to collaborate with and how to do that.

Ask yourself whether having the skills to develop a strategy to engage your stakeholders will help you to be more effective as a leader.

Change

In addition to mastering these first five key elements to becoming great at the *why* and *how* of leadership, it is essential for all leaders to be great at leading change. Change is the one thing that is constant in our *21st century* world.

There are two important truths here that will help you acknowledge this as a key part of your role as a leader. The first is that if an organization is changing less than the environment in which it operates it won't be sustainable. The second is that an organization can only change when the individual leaders change! This is why being able to lead change is a vital skill for you to develop as a sustainably effective leader.

If coping with change is a major challenge for you then I have written an extra chapter that you can download from my website as going into detail about change leadership has the potential to distract you from mastering the first five keys that you need to help you Stop Doing and Start Leading, and which are pre-requisites for being a great leader of change. Hence, I believe that a deep understanding of Change Leadership is outside the scope of this book.

Change is not easy and it fails more often than it succeeds. So would you agree that understanding how to catalyze change in yourself and others is an asset to both you and your organization?

Download the bonus chapter on leading change here: **https://suecoyne.com/stopdoingstartleading/**

These six areas make up the key developmental stages of transitioning from doing to leading.

As a result of incorporating these stages into my leadership development and coaching programs, I have experienced the joy of seeing leaders make this shift. When you Stop Doing and Start Leading you, like those who have already been on the journey before you, will be able to thrive in your own life and help your people thrive too. You will create your own ripple effect that impacts your organization and enhances the lives of your team, your family and everyone else you come into contact with. Being a leader is like a reverse virus, it spreads like wildfire and makes people feel great and be great.

So what impact will this have on you?

It means that you will have more balance as a person and will be more effective in all areas of your life. When you Stop Doing and Start Leading you'll have the time to take care of your own health and be there for people who matter in your life. You will also experience a sense of satisfaction and fulfillment that's just not possible when you are Doing and NOT Leading.

You and your people will thrive. Trust me when I tell you that you will enjoy a new level of motivation from seeing others grow because of you, and being able to do things they never dreamt they were capable of because of you. This creates the space for you to grow so that you continue to meet the needs of your organization. As a result, everyone will be able to make a greater contribution which, due to the law of cause and effect, means that your organization can continue to grow too. It means sustainable success for all and it's clear from all the people and organizations I have worked with that the impact is not only possible, but real and measurable.

You will be able to engage your stakeholders in a way that brings mutual success and enduring relationships.

You will know who you are as a leader and play your part in taking leadership into the 21st century.

So it's time to take the first step by looking at your identity as a leader.

STAGE ONE IDENTITY - REVEAL YOUR LEADERSHIP DNA

Chapter 3
Building Brand You

"The process of becoming a leader is not very different from that of becoming an integrated human being. A great leader is an integrated human being on a great mission, on a great journey to a better future. Don't fear this, take it on. This is the ultimate destiny of your passionate, powerful and confident self – the self you are uncovering/creating." - Warren Bennis

In this and the following chapters we will follow the journey of Frazzled Freda and see how she transitions from being a scientist to a great leader.

My intention in this chapter is to help you to identify what leadership means to you.

I'm going to help you to discover the answers to these vital questions and you'll understand why these questions are so important as you journey through this chapter:

- How do others see you?
- How do you see yourself?
- Do *you see* yourself as a leader?

To make the transition into being the great leader that you want to be it's important for you to know where you are now. It's vital to uncover *who you are* as a leader, and be clear about the difference that you want to make through your leadership. And, most importantly, to learn how you can **be** the leader you want to be.

Leadership Identity – Yes, it really matters!

Do you view your leadership as being rooted in your expertise?

What I've discovered is that for many leaders, their identity comes through their expertise – whether that's technical or professional. Often, when people come to me, they find themselves in a leadership role where they suddenly realize their expertise is no longer enough.

Maybe you have seen someone who has been promoted to a leadership role where they previously navigated their job based on their expertise then they suddenly find that they don't have the necessary skills to be an effective leader. You might have noticed that they showed signs of feeling vulnerable, as if they were on shaky ground. Maybe you have experienced those feelings yourself. I know I did when I was developing as a leader.

Let me introduce you to Emma. Emma's a finance expert who's recently been promoted to Finance Director. She has always prided herself on giving others the right answer to their questions and knowing the best way to do everything related to finances.

It's the morning of the management team meeting and Emma looks tired, bedraggled and anxious. She hasn't had time to wash her hair or iron her blouse. The meeting starts at 9am and she's spent all of last night racking her brains to think of answers to every possible question she might be asked. Deep down she's fearful that she might be floored.

Her team is sitting there watching and wondering why she doesn't trust them to do more and why she doesn't ask them to help her prepare for meetings. They feel frustrated that she isn't helping them to develop and that she has no time to help the team develop its strategy for the coming year. As she enters the meeting Emma has a knot in her stomach. What if Nigel asks her the one question she hasn't thought of?

Have you ever felt like that? Then you're stuck in the Expert Syndrome. Part and parcel of having the **Expert Syndrome** is that you believe that IQ is key. Whereas, in reality, IQ is a pre-requisite for a leader and it is emotional intelligence (EQ) that makes the difference between success and failure

Have you ever watched someone who has been promoted from being a manager to a position where they're expected to show leadership and watched as they struggle to be a leader? It's because they don't see *themselves* as a leader. So they can't be! Their identity, and therefore their mindset, is stuck in manager-mode. They have Manageritis.

So if you have Expert Syndrome or Manageritis, how do you overcome these ailments?

What does leadership mean to you?

The best way to start is undoubtedly to explore what leadership means to you.

What would you say is the difference between leadership and management? The views of a few leadership experts are summed up in the following table.

Leadership & Management

LEADERSHIP		MANAGEMENT
"Leadership is about nurturing and enhancing"	**Tom Peters**	*"Management is about arranging and telling."*
"Leaders are people who do the right thing"	**Warren Bennis**	*"Managers are people who do things right"*
"Leadership has about it a kinaesthetic feel, a sense of movement..."	**Kouzes and Posner**	*"Managing is about handling things, about maintaining order, about organisation and control."*
"Leaders are concerned about what things mean to people."	**Abraham Zaleznik**	*"Managers are concerned about how things get done."*
"Leaders are the architects."	**John Mariotti**	*"Managers are the builders."*

Take a few minutes to read the table. What you can see as you look at these different views is that managers focus on *efficiency* and what is happening *today*, whereas leaders focus on *effectiveness* and what is happening in the *future*. And as Warren Bennis (a pioneer in developing leadership thinking) says, leaders "do the right thing "whereas management is about "doing things right."

If you boil this down what you see is that leadership is about people and management is about things. Leadership is about the bigger picture and management is about the execution and the detail.

There is a general view amongst leadership experts that most organizations are over- managed and under- led. However, you can only lead people. Things such as money, costs, time, systems and processes all need to be managed. So, now you can see why organizations need both leadership and management to be successful.

An interesting question to reflect on is whether leadership and management can be present in the same person. What do you think?

In some cases I believe they can. The leaders I personally work with definitely feel that everybody needs a bit of both to be effective in their role, but some people major in leadership and others in management.

How do you balance leadership and management in your role? If you were as effective as you could possibly be in your role what would that balance be for you?

So, what is the basis on which people assume leadership? What I so often see is positional leadership that's based on power and authority: the 20th century version of leadership.

In the past, the reason we said that leadership was in short supply was that many of those who had been given positional authority to lead were actually bosses rather than leaders.

What would you say is the difference between a boss and a leader?

Well, as Theodore Roosevelt said, "The leader leads, and the boss drives."

The alternative is that leadership can be distributed to anyone in the organization, regardless of rank or role, who can show leadership in a given task or area. I believe that this distributed model of leadership is what's needed in modern organizations to reduce friction and improve performance.

What is required of great leaders today?

As Bob Geldof said, for many of us our definition of leadership is still stuck in the 20th century. Leadership is no longer about over -focusing on the bottom line. It is no longer about treating people as cogs in the machine and over working them so that they burn out from long-term stress. 21st century, sustainably effective leaders who have the skills to Stop Doing and Start Leading create a climate where their people can thrive so that the organization thrives. It is a more balanced, agile, emotionally intelligent style of leadership. But make no mistake, there's nothing soft and fluffy about emotionally intelligent leadership. Far from it. Creating an environment for sustainable high performance is based on a balance between challenging people and supporting them. It's not about Doing, it's about Leading.

Why forming your leadership DNA matters

So, let's bring this back to you now and to **your identity as a leader.**

You may say, "OK Sue, what if I don't know who I am as a leader? I don't even really know what you mean. How do I find out?"

From my experience of working with leaders since 2003 I have found that what most of them are missing is self-awareness in the context of leadership. So, of course, they don't know *who* they are as a leader (or sometimes in a wider context) because their identity comes from what they DO, not who they ARE.

The symptoms include not having a consistent way of behaving, which results in the people around them being unsure about what to expect from them. That means a chronic lack of trust. And who pulls the stops out for someone they don't trust? Do you expect to be able to trust someone yourself who doesn't trust themselves? I don't think so!

Maybe you recognize this in yourself. If you do, don't worry. You aren't alone.

You may remember me saying in an earlier chapter that trust in leaders is at an all-time low. Here are the facts on this: in the 2015 Edelman Trust Barometer, trust levels in business among the general public decreased in 16 of 27 countries. The majority of countries now sit below 50 percent with regard to trust in business. Sustainably effective, 21st century leaders have to start to reverse the low levels of trust people have in leaders. So how do you do it?

When I ask people in workshops what makes a great leader, a leader who has had an impact on them and their development, what do you think they say? They don't mention skill but instead they often mention being authentic as one of the top leadership attributes. One reason is that they can **trust** this person to do what is right for the team and the organization rather than just to focus on their own self-interests. Also, the fact that the leader has worked on their authenticity means that they have built a strong sense of self-identity and self-trust. That means they can be open about themselves. So, a key part of rebuilding trust involves leaders being seen as authentic, genuine and open.

That's the big picture reason why you need to know who you are as a leader so that you can be authentic and build trust. There's another reason why it's so important and it's much closer to home: not being authentic and being a totally different person at work is very stressful to maintain and will leave you feeling drained of energy and exhausted.

Authentic leadership – the difference that makes the difference

Authentic leaders are consistent and congruent. In other words, they walk their talk. Their beliefs, values and behaviors are aligned. What they say is congruent with their tone of voice and body language. Everything lines up and this level of authenticity only comes through your own self-awareness.

Authenticity is not only about self-awareness (though it is also about accepting yourself, warts and all); it's about accepting your strengths as well as your limitations. It comes from understanding your capabilities and being aware of your vulnerabilities.

This brings us back to the question we started to address earlier. What is leadership? Often your view of leadership means that it is ok to focus on strengths but you are not so comfortable about focusing on your limitations.

Isn't it true that in the past and in many cases still today many leaders feel that they need to *know* everything? Like Emma the FD, who worries about having to know everything, even the unknowable.

What is the result of having the belief that as a leader you need to know everything? Sleepless nights, stress and being seen as having "holes" in your knowledge. That's not a great recipe for not burning out is it?

So, the first question to ask yourself is this: is it actually possible to know everything?

I have coached many leaders who believed that to admit that they didn't know something was a sign of weakness. When I asked them what the impact of showing weakness would be they said that people would feel they weren't capable of doing their job. Which ultimately would mean they would lose their job. If they lost their job they would not be able to provide for their family. So, that one belief that a leader needs to know everything has massive implications. Feeling that you have to know everything has the potential to have an underlying feeling of fear driving everything you do.

So, what is the potential impact that your beliefs about leadership can have on you? How do leaders with the belief that they need to know everything get over it? I remember one struggling leader in particular. Reframing his definition of leadership liberated him. He was transformed when he decided to believe that being courageous was not about being a superhero but about having the courage to admit he didn't know something or that he could ask for help when he needed it. As a result of this new belief he changed his preparations for the monthly exec meeting to include asking his team for help and using their expertise to support him. He felt more energized and confident in that meeting and performed better. And here's the ripple effect it had: it also made his team feel more valued. So it was a win-win all round.

Within two months he was promoted.

Does your definition of leadership include being a superhero? What impact does believing you have to know everything have on your ability to learn from your mistakes? It's a negative spiral if you feel you do, and a positive one if you let go and get the support of others. When you Stop Doing (and Knowing) and Start Leading (and asking others for information and support) everything changes for the better. And how does all of this affect your ability to be authentic?

The truth is that the rapid pace of change in today's organizations means that no individual can possibly know everything and with the emphasis on failing fast there are three things leaders need to model:
- a willingness to be vulnerable
- being able to admit not knowing
- being able to admit having made a mistake

As the poet David Whyte puts it: "We need to learn to love the part of ourselves that limps."

Is leadership just about being authentic then?

Rob Goffee and Gareth Jones — in their book called *Why Should Anyone Be Led by You?*[2] — conclude that effective leadership isn't **just** about authenticity. Effective leadership is about authenticity **and** skill. Leaders who combine the two have authentic influence and create more value for their organizations and stakeholders.

Here's why it can be such a challenge for people. It's because it's much easier to improve your skills than it is to increase your authenticity. Increasing your authenticity requires going beyond what most business schools teach and takes a deeper level of learning. When I work with leaders my aim is to support them to become a great leader who has skills *and* authenticity.

The key learning for you to take out of this is that being a great leader is about being authentic in a way that is appropriate for the context you are operating in.

So, how do you develop this context- based authentic leadership? You do it by showing respect for the culture of your organization and acquiring just enough of the behaviors of the organization to be effective, without conforming to the culture so much, that you lose yourself and your own authenticity in the process.

So, ask yourself whether to be a great leader you need to have a reputation for authenticity.

This is not something that is going to happen overnight. It takes time.

Recently promoted Operations Director at Murray's Medical Molds, Frazzled Freda really hasn't got to grips with who she is as a leader yet. She came into science to make a difference. As a lab scientist, she had a clear vision of what that meant. As a senior leader she's feeling lost.

It's Sunday evening. Here's what's happening.

Sorting out Sam's school bag, Freda is feeling the familiar knot in her stomach tightening. When she was lead scientist, she'd always looked forward to Monday mornings. Not anymore. Time pressures are no longer the problem. She's been working with a coach on time management and has developed some useful new strategies. So, what is it that is making her feel so unhappy?

She is concerned that relationships with her team are deteriorating. On Friday, she got cross with Ian because he was late with some figures. He tried to explain, but she didn't give him the chance. She told herself it was her job as leader to be firm. After all, if she let him get away with it once wouldn't he push the boundaries further next time? Still, it hadn't felt quite right. So, when Sylvia, her PA, made more impossible diary arrangements, she just told her not to worry, these things happen. But that hadn't felt quite right either. Should she have done something different?

She is also still feeling uneasy about failing to push for an apprenticeship scheme. A few years back, she volunteered at a youth club. She knows how tough it can be for young people to get started and she feels strongly that employers have a responsibility to help. She hoped her promotion to Director would give her the chance to get a scheme started. When she sounded out a few of the other directors, though, she was met with unhelpful jokes about how useless young people are these days. As a result, she hasn't dared bring the subject up formally.

Then there are the meetings. Most of the people she now finds herself in meetings with are extroverts who are quick to speak. There is a lot of brainstorming with important decisions being made at a pace, which seems to her to be rash. She is much more analytical. Typically, insights come to her a day or two later, when she's had the chance to reflect on the discussions. She recognizes that these insights are often valuable but doesn't know what to do to get them shared.

Sighing, she puts Sam's homework picture in his bag, scoops him into bed and starts to read him his bedtime story. For her own bedtime reading she's set aside a research paper from this month's

Medical Molds Today. There's a meeting on the topic first thing Monday morning. She can't risk someone asking her a question she doesn't have the answer to.

How to develop a reputation for being authentic

I help people to create what I refer to as their own Authentic Leadership Brand. This simple idea has helped many of my leadership clients to become effective, authentic leaders. It has an especially powerful impact on women leaders who often have started with less confidence. Women are more able to confidently and positively position themselves as a leader and to put themselves forward for promotion when traditionally they are less inclined than men to do so.

One female leader I worked with had recently been promoted to a leadership position. She had been with the company a long time and had worked her way up. She was in her thirties and felt that other leaders saw her as young and inexperienced, while former colleagues did not see her as a leader but as one of them. Focusing on her leadership brand helped her to position herself as the leader she now was. She said this:

"I use the Authentic Leadership Brand to help keep me on track. It has really helped me to step into this role and feel more confident, and to have a vision for my future which gives me the desire and confidence to keep growing."

Developing your personal **Authentic Leadership Brand** provides a framework to develop your self-awareness and self-identity. Your authentic leadership brand underpins everything you do to build credibility. It helps you to build trust, enrich your relationships, master yourself, unblock your potential and develop your self-esteem. It is your personal positioning strategy. It is how you manage and influence how others perceive you. It is the vehicle through which you create value for yourself and others by performing in a sustainable way over the long term.

Developing your Authentic Leadership Brand takes courage and effort as it involves really getting to know who you are on the inside. Aspects that you need to explore are your strengths, what you are passionate about, your values, what you would like your legacy to be and what the purpose of your leadership and possibly your life is.

Let's explore these areas a little so that you understand why they are important to your authentic leadership brand.

Strengths

Looking at your strengths is a positive place to start to build your self-awareness. How aware are you of your strengths? How comfortable do you feel talking about them? Some people are uncomfortable talking about their strengths because they have been brought up not to be arrogant or to brag about themselves. They are also uncomfortable because in the workplace we have had such an emphasis over the last decade on identifying weaknesses. However, the work by Martin Seligman in Positive Psychology is proving to us that working with strengths is often the most effective way to get the best out of people, including ourselves.

Passions

Passion is not always encouraged in a corporate setting is it? How much of your passion do you bring into work each day? The fact that passion is not encouraged in corporate life is regrettable as it's what makes people feel alive and want to really make a contribution. I recall working with leaders in two different major global corporations who saved their passion for what they did outside of work. This ranged from kayaking to contributing to their local community by being on committees. What a loss for their organization!

Take a moment to think about something you are passionate about. Really imagine that you are involved in whatever it is that you are thinking about. What do you notice about how it makes you feel?

Passion makes you feel more engaged. It helps you to generate enthusiasm, enjoyment and inspiration. Passion is the fuel that drives things forward. It gives you the power that you need to achieve an outcome that you care deeply about. You can't do without it.

Sometimes our passion gets blocked. How can we overcome these passion blocks? One of the fastest ways to unlock your natural passion is to become clear on what you want and why. Working on your Authentic Leadership Brand will definitely help with this.

You may have heard people say "follow your passion," but you have to find it before can follow it!

Values

All individuals have their own set of personal values. What are values? Your values are very deeply held and are often at an unconscious level as they are formed throughout your life from birth to adulthood. Therefore, it's not always easy to identify them. They are like tree branches with our related beliefs and attitudes hanging from them like leaves. They act as our personal compass and influence the choices we make and the way we behave. You can't alter your attitudes and your behaviors unless you understand what drives them and what drives them are your inner values.

Vision

Once you have identified your strengths, passions and values you are ready to open things out and start to look at your vision. This answers the question, Why? for you. You start by asking yourself questions like: Why am I doing what I am doing? What direction do I want to go in?

As a leader within your organization you need to create a compelling vision for your people and you also need a vision for your Authentic Leadership Brand. This vision should paint an inspiring picture of the future that you want to create through your leadership, the destination you are heading for.

It will most likely go beyond your organizational leadership role and encompass your leadership of your life and be what will bring you fulfillment.

The poet and philosopher David Whyte has an inspirational way of thinking about this that you might want to consider as a frame of reference for creating your Authentic Leadership Brand vision. He says that we have three marriages[3] in life: to our significant other, our work and to ourselves. Rather than think about work-life balance and have competition between these different marriages, he advocates the notion of creating a vision and purpose big enough to hold them all equally, a "marriage of marriages".

A great leader leaves a legacy; you could say that they leave their footprints on the road for others to follow. So, developing your brand vision will undoubtedly require you to reflect on the legacy you want to leave. This links into one of our deepest drives as human beings: to make a contribution.

How does it make you feel when you are making a real contribution? What I have seen in organizations is that when people feel as if they're contributing they gain a profound sense of meaning and purpose.

How do you feel when you are not contributing? Not being able to contribute causes us to feel lost and unfulfilled. We sense that nothing really matters and, worse still, that we don't matter.

What if simply being authentic, being your best and fully expressing your strengths, talents and abilities were all it took to make a contribution to the world? The thing to remember is that this is true; being your best inspires others and can and does make an impact.

Purpose

Once you have articulated your vision you are ready to move onto your Purpose. Your Purpose is what you need to concentrate on in order to bring your vision to reality. It is also about how you need to grow and develop in order to realize your vision. It is not easy to articulate your purpose; the chances are it won't come to you immediately but will gradually emerge. If you would like some help in developing your brand go to **https://suecoyne.com/stopdoing startleading/** and get free access to a workbook on creating your Authentic Leadership Brand.

With all this in place you are ready to develop your **Authentic Leadership Brand Statement**. This is like the strapline of your brand. Its aim is to inform and inspire people so it needs to be clear and easy to understand. It is not the same thing as your Vision and Purpose, which are longer-term concepts.

Managing Your Authentic Leadership Brand

Many leaders take the time to develop an Authentic Leadership Brand but most don't manage it effectively. To get the return on your investment in creating your Authentic Leadership Brand you need to take control of it and the messages it sends to others in order to position yourself appropriately.

Your Authentic Leadership Brand will give you a sense of your identity as a leader. It will also start to build your confidence in yourself as a leader.

Reflection space

How would you rate yourself out of 10 (where 10 is the best score) for being an authentic leader?

Why does it matter if you have a reputation for authenticity?

What one insight have you got from this chapter that you wish to try out?

Chapter 4
Growing Your Confidence – Become an Energizer!

Magnificent You

Our deepest fear is not that we are inadequate
Our deepest fear is that we are powerful beyond measure
It is our light, not our darkness that most frightens us
We ask ourselves, "Who am I to be so brilliant, gorgeous, talented
and fabulous?"
Actually, who are you not to be?
You are a child of God
Your playing small doesn't serve the world
There is nothing enlightened about shrinking so that other people
won't feel insecure around you
We are all meant to shine, as children do
We were born to make manifest the glory that is within us
It is not just in some of us, it is in everyone
And as we let our own light shine, we unconsciously
Give others permission to do the same
As we are liberated from our fear, our presence
Automatically liberates others
Marianne Williamson[4]

45

My intention in this chapter is to help you to understand what prevents you from being confident as a leader and how you can put in place a self-support system that ensures you are a confident leader most of the time.

What is confidence?

Confidence is about trust, courage, optimism and resilience.

What do we mean when we say that confidence is about trust? It's simply the ability to trust yourself. Self-confidence requires self-trust at a number of levels including:

- trusting in your ability to do something or take certain actions
- trusting that you won't let yourself down

What do we mean when we say confidence is about courage? Courage gives you the confidence to take appropriate and effective action in any situation, however challenging it appears to you.

What does optimism have to do with confidence? You are able to accept negative feedback from others while remaining focused on your own positive outcomes.

What does resilience have to do with confidence? When you have healthy self-confidence you are able to cope with setbacks without being knocked off course.

It's important to point out that it's not about being over-confident or arrogant. Many of us have been brought up to believe that it is wrong to self-promote or be arrogant. Sometimes this belief gets in our way and stops us from allowing ourselves to be appropriately confident for fear of being seen as arrogant.

How does confidence affect leadership?

What I know is that for most of the leaders I work with, improving their confidence as a leader is high on the agenda. They recognize that a lack of self-confidence really limits their effectiveness as a leader.

Confidence is something that recently-promoted Operations Director Freda had in abundance in her former lead scientist role, but which seems to be eluding her in her new position. What's gone wrong?

Let's take a look back at Freda's teenage years.

At school, Freda had always been seen as one of the geeky ones. She'd only really felt she fitted in when she was in her (always top set) science classes. Elsewhere, she'd often been teased as a swot. Teachers hadn't always been helpful, either. Too many of them liked to put the children into boxes and she was firmly in the analytical scientist kid box. She wasn't expected to be creative or to have interesting ideas on broader topics. And because it tended to take time for her to formulate her thoughts she'd consistently fulfilled the teachers' low expectations by failing to come up with anything worthwhile to say in classroom discussions outside the science block.

While most of her teachers simply moved on to the next student after getting little response from Freda, one or two preferred ritual humiliation. Mr. Gregory, her 3rd year history teacher, was the worst. He'd taken a sadistic delight in picking on her first, asking what she thought and criticizing her brief responses. "A bright girl like you, Freda – is that all you can come up with?" or "Do you really think that's the only reason?"

Had Freda's teachers been more patient, they would have discovered her analytical skills supported a creative and insightful mind – just the combination of qualities, in fact, that were later to make her both stand out as a scientist and be spotted as potential director material. But, little by little, she'd grown to believe that she really didn't have much to contribute outside of science classes – though learning the facts was no problem.

Freda doesn't have the self-awareness to spot that her lack of confidence as a leader comes from self-limiting beliefs she developed growing up. She's not confident she has anything worthwhile to say outside the scientific environment and she's scared of being seen as stupid. She's not at all unusual. She knows that confidence is key to effective leadership – what she hasn't yet realized is that it starts and ends with what's inside her own head.

As a leader are you an energy drainer or an energizer?

A key message is that confidence as a leader does not come from having a particular expertise or from your knowledge. It comes mainly from self-awareness and self-management.

What impact does a confident leader have on those around them? Confident leaders have positive focused energy, they are happy with themselves and with life. This positivity is contagious and energizes people.

What impact does a leader who lacks confidence have on those around them? Leaders who lack confidence drain energy from the people around them.

What affects your confidence?

Confidence can change in different situations. Perhaps, like Freda, you were more confident in your previous role than you are in your current one. How many people do you know who are confident in all areas of their life? I don't know many people like that.

Confidence can be affected by the attitude of others towards you or the situation you find yourself in. **But the biggest determinant of how confident you feel as a leader is your attitude towards yourself.**

How can you support your self-confidence?

When we talk about the area of confidence there are lots of words beginning with self, such as self-awareness. It is difficult to know exactly what they all mean. In this section, we will explore the seven most important ones that can be addressed to support your self-confidence.

1. Self–awareness

The first way that you can support your confidence is by developing your self-awareness. What do we mean by self-awareness in this context? Well, it is about being aware of your strengths and of your limitations and acknowledging them. This is part of getting to know and understanding yourself. It boosts your resilience and ability to take on greater challenges. Are you able to acknowledge both your strengths and your limitations?

2. Self-acceptance

What you need to be able to acknowledge your strengths and limitations is a good level of self-acceptance. It means that you accept and love yourself exactly as you are, warts and all. You are able to recognize your weaknesses, limitations and idiosyncrasies without this interfering with your ability to fully accept yourself. As such, self-acceptance is unconditional.

What happens if you don't have it?

Have you ever experienced a time when there was a judgmental, critical voice inside your head? What impact does that judgmental, critical voice have on your confidence? Maybe you compare yourself to others and feel inferior.

Negatively comparing yourself to others can have a very negative impact and we rarely think about the likelihood of those very people doing exactly the same thing to themselves. Think about that for a moment. They might even be comparing themselves to you!

Many of us limit ourselves by letting our inner critic affect our confidence and the choices we make in life. Your inner dialogue influences how you feel about yourself and how you behave, so it is worth taking the time to change it from being an inner critic to being an inner sponsor.

Becoming our own sponsor involves a shift in mindset. It's about realizing that self-acceptance has nothing to do with achievements, it's not something that you have to earn through your hard work nor is self-acceptance something you get as a result of being the best. These are the standards of perfectionism that make self-acceptance conditional rather than unconditional. As such they are not supportive of your self-confidence.

On the other hand, it does not stop you from wanting to grow and develop. Accepting yourself as you are today doesn't mean you won't have the motivation to make changes or improvements that will make you more effective or that will enrich your life and probably the lives of others as well. As Dr. Carol Dweck explains in her book *Mindset*[5] this is about having a growth mind-set and seeing yourself as a work in progress.

So, to sum up it helps you to see that self-acceptance is unconditional and you don't have to *do* anything to secure it. It also requires you to see yourself as a work in progress.

Your level of self-acceptance is down to you and no-one else. Once you decide to stop *judging* yourself and negatively comparing yourself to others you get in touch with your compassion for yourself and your ability to accept that you are doing the best you can with the resources you have.

Are you diminishing your self-confidence by being your own worst critic or supporting it by being your own sponsor?

3. Self-image

Some people say that confidence is almost all about perception and you have just seen that how you view yourself influences your level of self-acceptance. So, you could say that how you see yourself is how you will show up. This brings us to self-image.

Your self-image is the foundation upon which your life is built. The way you think about yourself determines everything you do, say, believe and feel. So, the world around you is a reflection of your inner world.

So what image do you have of yourself?

A common problem that makes some people very unhappy is having an unrealistic image of themselves. It could be based on having unsuitable role models that you try to emulate rather than being your authentic self.

What expectations do you have of yourself?

Some leaders lack confidence in doing anything because they are afraid that they will say something stupid or do something wrong that will humiliate them.

Why would someone have those fears? One reason is if they have a limiting belief that they have to be perfect. Imagine trying to live up to that. Imagine how terrifying it is. How would that make you feel about yourself? Isn't it true that every human being makes mistakes? Isn't it also true that we all do silly things at times?

Learning to accept the fact that you are human with flaws and faults is more appropriate. It means that you see making mistakes and errors as normal and you don't beat yourself up for it. Of course, you learn from them so that you don't keep making the same mistakes over and over again. Learning to laugh at yourself when you do something silly or when you say something amiss is being human. This allows you to admit your mistakes and shortcomings and do it with a smile. It means that you are not afraid to say "I don't know".

Let me tell you about Amy. Amy had been promoted to Customer Service Manager. She's young and has been promoted ahead of people who have been in the organization much longer than her. When we looked at why she wasn't feeling confident in her new role we discovered that she had a fear of being found out. She felt that she had to be instantly perfect in the new role otherwise others would think that she wasn't capable of it and didn't deserve it. This is commonly called The Imposter Syndrome and is quite prevalent in women leaders. Through the coaching Amy was able to shift her mind-set and start to believe that she had been selected for her job because her company believed she would do it well. It's not realistic to expect to have all the knowledge on day one.

So, self-confidence is enhanced when you have realistic expectations of yourself. Make a mental check to see whether the image you have of yourself is boosting or sapping your confidence.

4. Self-esteem

Self-awareness, self-acceptance and self-image all contribute to our self-esteem. Self-esteem is key to your confidence because it is how you value yourself and how worthwhile you regard yourself to be.

People with healthy self-esteem:

- Have a quiet confidence
- They don't fish for compliments but they do accept them as they know what they are worth
- They may be quite humble
- They recognize and are often interested in other people and their achievements
- They may not be bothered about receiving external recognition
- They are often relaxed, upright, calm, measured, decisive and don't hesitate.
- They make good eye contact

Self-esteem can be problematical either if it is too high or if it is too low. An over-emphasis on self-esteem can result in pumping yourself up and becoming "grandiose". Someone with this sort of grandiosity will:

- Boast
- Show off
- Name-drop
- Hog the conversation
- Tell you all about their achievements

Low self-esteem is founded on negative self-beliefs. These beliefs originate from negative judgments about ourselves, which we see as facts and which then become beliefs. We interpret every life event as evidence to support our negative self-beliefs. These beliefs are often opinions, not facts. They could be based on others' opinions or negative experiences we have had. People with low self-esteem consistently underachieve because they underestimate themselves or feel unworthy.

How did these negative beliefs develop? Most of your beliefs were in place by the time you were seven-years-old and are hard-wired into your long term memory. There are four aspects to the development of these negative self-beliefs:

- During our early years we have experiences that create ideas about "self" such as rejection, neglect or being the "odd one out" which lead to...

- The core belief. This is an assessment of our worth or value as a person and might lead to other beliefs such as "I am worthless" or "I am not good enough" which lead to...

- The development of our guidelines for coping or survival; "I must avoid this," "I must always put others first," "if I am myself I will be rejected," which lead to...

- Trigger situations. These are situations in which our guidelines are transgressed resulting in defensiveness and feelings of rejection, failure or being out of control.

So, what you can see is that your early experiences and the limiting beliefs they create not only remain unchallenged into adulthood, but also generate self-reinforcing and self-fulfilling mechanisms that are regularly triggered.

It's also been discovered that our brains have something called neuroplasticity. Neuroplasticity allows us to recover from certain types of brain injury and even re-route our brain signals to do certain things. The human brain has the capacity to re-wire itself. It is physically possible to alter your thinking, your beliefs and therefore to improve levels of self-esteem and confidence. The starting place is to identify any limiting beliefs you have now. The next step is to develop a more supportive set of beliefs for yourself and set about hard-wiring them. When you do this you immediately start to reverse the self-fulfilling negativity of low self-esteem.

Healthy self-esteem is built up layer by layer through healthy beliefs, through not being so hard on yourself, through liking yourself as a total package and through feeling justifiable pride in your achievements. It is difficult to have self-confidence without self-esteem, so it is worth taking the time to work on whatever is required to build healthy levels of self-esteem.

5. Self-efficacy

Self-efficacy is the strength of your belief in your own ability to complete tasks and reach goals. High and low self-efficacy determine whether or not someone will choose to take on a challenging task or "write it off" as impossible. Self-efficacy builds confidence through getting something right, understanding why it is right and being able to replicate it. The concept of self-efficacy was developed by Albert Bandura and is linked to resilience and overcoming obstacles.

How does your current level of self-efficacy affect your resilience and ability to overcome obstacles and setbacks? Could it be improved?

6. Self-support

Many of the people I coach who have low self-confidence think that the solution is to get more encouragement and praise from those around them. As you move higher up the organization this happens less and less so it is vital if you are to be a sustainably effective leader to recognize that it is your responsibility to support and nurture your own self-confidence.

I often use the metaphor that your confidence is like seeds that you have planted in your garden. If you want those seeds to grow and blossom into flowers you need to water and nourish them. This is exactly what you need to do to enable your self-confidence to flourish.

Another limiting belief we are often brought up with is that it is wrong to be selfish and put yourself first. We are taught to put others first. What is the impact of this belief? What many of the leaders I coach come to realize is that if they don't start to put themselves first they will not be able to serve others in the way that they want to.

What happens when you put yourself at the bottom of the pile? You send a message to yourself that you are less worthy and important than others. This can build resentment, ill health and unhappy relationships. The truth is that in order to support other people you need to be generous to yourself first.

This is about taking the time to create a positive environment in which you can thrive and be at your best. You can't do this for others until you do it for yourself.

This will be a model to others to show that they also can do this for themselves and not be dependent on you for it.

Are you undermining your self-confidence or nurturing it so that you can thrive and enable others to do so too?

7. Self-actualization

**Self-Actualisation –
Maslow's Hierarchy of Needs**

Self-actualisation
Personal growth and fulfilment

Esteem needs
Achievement, status, responsibility, reputation

Belongingness and Love needs
Family, affection, relationships, work group

Safety needs
Protection, security, order, law, limits, stability

Biological and Physiological needs
Basic needs – air, food, drink, shelter, warmth, sex, sleep

Abraham Maslow developed his Hierarchy of Needs[6] in 1943. At the top of this pyramid of needs is self-actualization. Maslow described this as the desire for self-fulfillment – the desire to become everything you are capable of becoming.

Confidence is a milestone towards self-actualization; it comes in the esteem box on the pyramid although it is only possible once you have found love and a sense of belonging, which are below it on the hierarchy which in turn are only possible once you have safety.

What does self-actualization mean in the context of effective leadership? It means realizing your full potential. It is about self-mastery. It is also about acknowledging that you are here for a bigger purpose and having the courage to grow so that you can step up to that purpose.

What would be the impact if you followed the sentiment in the poem at the start of this chapter?

What you need to remember is that your mindset determines whether you lose or gain confidence.

What impact will building your confidence have?

The chances are that as you act on building your self-confidence others will notice obvious changes in your attitude and your behaviors. They may well experience you as calmer and able to manage stress well. They may also notice that you are enjoying your role as a leader more, that you are able to adapt according to the situation you find yourself in.

Reflection space

How would you currently score your overall level of confidence as a leader out of 10 (where 10 is the best score)?

Why is it important to have a high confidence score?

What is one insight that you are taking from this chapter?

STAGE TWO BALANCE – THE THREE H'S OF A BALANCED LEADER

Chapter 5
The Zero Burnout Strategy for
Your Balanced Leadership

"My mission in life is not merely to survive but to thrive; and to do so with some passion, some compassion, some humor and some style." – Dr. Maya Angelou

Balance comes in threes

I believe that in the 21st century leaders who create climates in which they and their people risk burn-out will not only be unfit to lead, they will no longer fit in. They will become out-dated and obsolete.

So what is the definition of success that will enable leaders and their people to thrive in this new world?

To answer this question we need to first look at the organizations in which leaders are operating. Organizations and the people in them are living systems that do not operate in isolation. They are part of a much bigger system.   The complex global system on which organizations depend for their survival and success is made up of the natural environment, the social and political system and the global economy and is referred to as the **Triple Context**. The collapse of any one of these would result in the collapse of the others. They are inter-dependent.

What is the definition of organizational success that takes this **Triple Context** into account?

It is the **Triple Bottom Line** (TBL), coined by John Elkington in 1994. This consists of three Ps: profit, people and planet. It is, in effect, a balanced scorecard. Many organizations such as Unilever and DSM follow Triple Bottom Line reporting.

For organizations to thrive in the 21st century and be able to perform consistently well across all aspects of this more balanced definition of success, they will need a new breed of leader who can bring balance to their own lives and deliver sustainable high performances.

Would you agree with me that the current definition of success for most leaders is how well they are delivering their financial objectives and the compensation package they receive as a result? This causes many leaders to work long hours and to lack balance in their lives.

As I found out, working long hours consistently over a long period of time is not sustainable. It leads to exhaustion and burnout, which have an impact not only on your performance at work but also on all aspects of your life.

Having coached many leaders since 2003, I realize that they are no different to most other people. There are three things that most people want in their life: happiness, health and success. The trick is to find a way of living your life that allows all three to co-exist.

This realization led me to create **Triple H Leadership** to support leaders in adopting a wider definition of success based on being a happy, healthy and high performing leader.

Imagine living your life according to this wider definition so that you have time to look after your health, to do things that make you happy and to spend time with the people who matter most to you. Imagine what a difference that would make to how you feel at work and therefore the sort of climate you would create at work. You ensure that you continue to grow and develop your leadership skills so that you energize, engage and empower your people. You show that you believe in them and support them in growing to do things they didn't imagine they were capable of. Your relationships outside of work start to thrive as well because you are not constantly stressed and thinking about work, meaning you have quality time with your friends and family. You make the time to think strategically and to develop your understanding of the organization beyond your own department so you can contribute more widely and add more value.

Having this wider definition of success is what gives you balance and sustainable success in all areas of your life.

Murray's Medical Molds Operations Director Freda left the management meeting with a frown on her face. She'd hoped to be out of work at 5pm that evening, but Tony, the MD, wanted an urgent update on the protocol alignment project. He'd found some inconsistencies in her latest report. She couldn't understand how she hadn't spotted them herself. She never used to make mistakes.

Freda's frown was fast becoming a permanent feature. There was just so much to worry about. Her team didn't help. When she'd first taken over there had been a buzz in the department and performance levels were high. But that hadn't lasted. She couldn't work out why. Didn't they understand how important it was to meet targets? She kept the pressure up but it wasn't working. Instead, both Ian, her deputy, and several others were off work with bugs and things were falling even further behind.

Walking back to her desk, Freda passed her colleague, Effective Ellie. Ellie had been for a run with a few of her team members and they were chatting as they headed for the showers. Freda knew Ellie and, like her, was working on a number of big projects. How could she spare the time for exercise and how could she seem so relaxed? It didn't seem fair. Ellie's team all seemed such a happy bunch too and they had a reputation for getting the job done.

As she sat down Freda heard a text come in and checked her phone. It was her friend Cassie suggesting they meet up for a drink. Sighing, Freda texted back an immediate excuse. She couldn't see how she'd have the time. She tried to remember when she'd last spoken to Cassie or, in fact, to any of her friends. It was probably at least six weeks ago.

As for actually meeting up socially with anyone, the last time would have been that Sunday lunch with her cousin John and his family back before Christmas. But that was OK. Work had to be the priority, just for the moment. Once the big projects she was working on were out of the way things would be different.

Over the course of the afternoon Freda started to feel another of her regular headaches coming on. She hadn't had time for lunch but that was nothing unusual.

Freda finally left the office at 6.30. She'd planned to go shopping to get some decent food for dinner but went straight home instead to make sure she had time to see her son Sam before bed. They'd just have to eat pizza from the freezer again. She'd have to finish work earlier and make it to the supermarket the next day. Sam was already in his pajamas when she got back so she took him up to bed and started to read him a story. Ten minutes later she was fast asleep.

So, read on to find out the strategies that make the difference. Now it's time to explore the three H's of high performance, health and happiness.

Chapter 6
Creating the Time and Energy to Lead

"The key is not to prioritize what's on your schedule but to schedule your priorities." - Stephen R Covey

I believe there are two precious resources that are key to our ability to be sustainable high performers – energy and time. You need to become good at managing both.

Managing your energy

I use this Performance Zone model to talk to leaders about managing their energy and being resilient so they are available to energize their people.

Personal Energy Management

Stress Zone		Peak Performance Zone	
※ Frustration		※ Centred	※ Creative
※ Anxiety		※ Happy	※ Flow
※ Anger		※ Present	※ Energised
※ Fear		※ Effortless	※ Inspired
※ Irritation		※ Alive	※ Balanced
※ Unbalanced		※ Powerful	
Burn Out Zone		**Re-energise Zone**	
※ Exhausted		▪ Relaxed	
※ Apathetic		▪ Peaceful	
※ Listless		▪ Calm	
※ Dis-ease		▪ Still	
※ Lifeless		▪ At ease	
※ Helpless		▪ In your body	

How often are you performing at your peak? How does it feel when you are at your best, in the peak performance zone on the diagram above? When I ask this question people give me the sort of positive emotions shown in the top right-hand box of the diagram. There is no doubt that it feels good to be in this zone.

Often, when operating in this peak performance zone you are in a state of flow. The term "flow" was first used by Mihaly Csikszentmihalyi in his book *Flow: The Psychology of Optimal Experience*[7] which was published in 1990. He described flow as "being completely involved in an activity for its own sake. The ego falls away. Time flies. Every action, movement and thought follows inevitably from the previous one, like playing jazz. Your whole being is involved and you are using your skills to the utmost". Flow is essential for the highest levels of performance.

Many leaders would dearly love to operate in the zone of peak performance more often. However, it is important to remember that we are living systems. We are not computers and we don't operate in a linear way; we can't run continuously at high speeds for long periods of time, running multiple programs at the same time. That is unsustainable for us.

Yet, because of the mechanistic view in many organizations we are expected to perform at a high level 95 percent of the time. If we compare this to athletes we see that they are only expected to perform at their best for 5 percent of the time. The rest of the time they are in training or recovery. Nowadays sleep; meditation and napping are incorporated into the training of elite athletes. This is because it has been shown that as a result they recover faster and perform better.

Our body tells us when it needs re-energizing and recovery.

How often do you override what your body needs? How often do you grab a coffee or cigarette, some food or chocolate to keep you going? Over the long -term it is not healthy to ignore our body in this way. Recovery builds energy so it builds our resistance when things get really bad. If we are not giving ourselves space during the day it doesn't help us to be at our best or help our brains to be creative.

How often during the working day do you take some time out to re-energize? For most people this leaves them feeling peaceful and calm. It enables them to be at their best more of the time.

How could you fit more time to re-energize into your day? One suggestion is that you set the alarm on your phone for every one to two hours and take a short break. In the break you could drink some water, do a two-minute mindfulness exercise, practice breathing deeply or have a short walk. Explore all of these and see which ones energize you the most and help you to feel more in touch with yourself.

A good day begins the night before so a vital part of your recovery program is making sure you get enough sleep.

When demands exceed capacity and there is more energy going out than coming in we go into the **stress zone** – the top left box in the diagram. Some leaders I have worked with say that they spend as much as 65 percent of their time in this zone. People tend to feel negative emotions when in this zone such as frustration, anxiety, anger and fear. Due to these negative emotions it is highly likely that when we are in this zone we are in fight/flight/freeze mode. This stress response shuts down our pre-frontal cortex, which means we aren't able to perform at our best. Not only that, our bodies are flooded with stress hormones, cortisol and adrenaline. Our stress response mechanism is meant to be short-lived and it is not good for us to have the stress hormones in our bodies over a sustained period of time. If this happens there is a danger we will go into the **burnout zone** (bottom left on the diagram).

When you are running on empty you can't cope, you are reactive and you make bad decisions. You are very transactional and just want to cross things off your to-do list, which means that you miss unexpected problems and issues.

This place of exhaustion and listlessness is not a good place to be at all. Stress and burnout diminish performance for most people. You will undoubtedly know of people who have succeeded despite their burnout. You have to ask yourself though how much joy and pleasure they could have experienced if they had come from a place of flow?

So, if you are to avoid stress and burnout and be at your best more of the time you need to build recovery breaks into your working day and make sure you get enough sleep.

I am noticing that attitudes are changing concerning this. We are in the midst of a transition from the mind-set that you can't succeed without burning out to a place where people accept the science, which is showing that this is completely untrue. It is now obvious that burnout not only generally inhibits performance but also has an adverse effect on the bottom line over the long term. What is more, it destroys people's health causing health care costs to increase due to preventable stress- related illnesses. As a result, some organizations are starting to act more responsibly by introducing stress reduction and stress management programs into the workplace.

Making the right time choices

This is the second aspect of being a sustainably high performer.

Many of the leaders I coach are overwhelmed when they come to me because they are too focused on day-to-day activities and too involved in detail. As a result, they feel under pressure and are unable to find the time to lead their people and focus on strategy.

Feeling overwhelmed is a sure sign that we have gone off track and need to course correct. Having a sense of time famine and experiencing breathlessness are indicators that we are not making effective time choices.

Neuroscience reveals some surprises

Our working memory has limited capacity

Sometimes leaders focus on the detail or day-to-day because that is what they are used to doing – it is comfortable and has become a habit. It takes less energy to do things that have become habitual, as they are hardwired in our brain. Learning to do new or less familiar things takes more energy as we have to create a new neural pathway which requires repetition before it gets hardwired and becomes a habit.

There is no such thing as good multitasking

The myth is that women are better than men at multitasking. The truth is that we can all only focus on one conscious task at a time. We are more effective when we mono-task and are infinitely faster. Doing multiple tasks results in a big drop in accuracy or performance. Also, switching between tasks uses energy and if you do this a lot you can make mistakes. Multitasking is easier if it involves executing embedded routines. However, if as a result of constant multitasking at work you have *continuous partial attention* you will find that you experience constant and intense mental exhaustion.

Neuroscience proves it – Your brain power has energy limits

Certain important activities such as prioritizing take up a lot of energy. The reason prioritizing is hard is because it involves imagining and moving around concepts of which you have no direct experience. It also involves understanding new ideas as well as making decisions, remembering and inhibiting all at once – it is like the triathlon of mental tasks or like skiing a black run. So, you need to do it when you are fresh and energized. Hence, you need to carefully consider what you spend your limited mental resources on.

You need to schedule tasks requiring the most attention and energy when you have a fresh and alert mind. Deep thinking requires more effort, so plan to do it in one block early in the morning or late at night.

Get disciplined about *not thinking* when you don't have to. Don't pay attention to non-urgent tasks unless or until it is truly necessary.

Another technique for thinking less about unnecessary tasks is to delegate them well. Delegating also uses up a lot of energy so it is best done with a fresh mind.

Distractions drain your energy

Every time you allow yourself to be distracted by a call or e-mail it takes more effort to focus and you have lower energy reserves to draw on. Distractions are not just frustrating but can be exhausting and result in you making mistakes on important tasks, forgetting good ideas and losing valuable insights. You need to manage distractions by switching off all communication devices when doing thinking work. Even internal thoughts can be distractions so clear your mind before embarking on difficult tasks.

Maintaining a good focus requires you to inhibit the wrong things from coming into focus. The process of inhibiting happens in the pre-frontal cortex and is a limited resource. Each time you stop yourself from doing something the next impulse is harder to stop. When you are tired, hungry or anxious it is harder to inhibit the wrong impulses. To inhibit distractions and stay focused you need to be aware of your internal mental processes and catch the wrong impulses before they take hold. You must veto them before they turn from impulse to action.

A study done at London University found that constant e-mail and text-messaging reduces mental capacity by an average of 10 points on an IQ test. The effect is similar to missing a night's sleep and I have already mentioned how important a good night's sleep is to being a sustainably effective leader.

Being "always on" is not a productive way to work as the brain is forced to be "on alert" far too much which results in more stress hormones in your body which can ultimately adversely affect your health.

I have used this learning from neuroscience to develop **five key steps to creating the time to lead and be strategic.** I produced this "Time to Lead Guide" for my clients who find it a practical and useful tool to help them. You can get your complimentary copy from **https://suecoyne.com/stopdoingstartleading/**

The latest thinking from neuroscience makes it really clear that you need to identify your absolute priorities or vital few so that you free up the time you need to spend on leading your team, on focusing your energy where you can have the most impact and on adding strategic value to your organization. As you do this you will notice the effect this has on the positive impact you are having on your people, and the difference you are making. Your work/life balance will improve significantly too.

Reflection space

How would you rate yourself at managing your energy out of 10 (where 10 is the best score)?

How would you rate yourself at making effective time choices out of 10 (where 10 is the best score)?

Why does it matter to do both of these things well?

What insights have you got from this chapter that you want to try out?

Chapter 7
Being a Healthy Leader

"There is no trade-off between taking care of yourself and achieving – you don't have to choose between them." *- Arianna Huffington*[8]

Why focus on health?

Have you heard the saying health is wealth? What we mean when we say this is that your health is your main asset. Without it you don't have anything else. Think about Steve Jobs, former CEO of Apple Inc. – he became a billionaire but he is no longer with us because money can't buy you health.

As someone who has experienced a serious health scare, I feel qualified to say that your health matters and is fundamental to you being a sustainably effective leader. If you don't Stop Doing and Start Leading your health will be at risk!

What I experienced is that without good health the future is uncertain; in fact, often you can't even see a future at all. With good health you feel full of energy and vitality and feel that anything is possible.

Experiencing health problems is a wake-up call to change how you are living your life, and very often there's no warning. As I said earlier, one of the reasons I became a coach was to help leaders to find a more balanced, sustainable way of leading so that they didn't have to experience the sort of wake-up call that hit me and many other leaders I know. That's what I want for you and hopefully what you want for yourself.

I believe that being given a leadership role is a privilege and an honor. It is an opportunity to really have an impact and make your difference. The instrument through which you make your difference is you. So, does it make sense that you need to take care of that instrument? I think so.

Taking responsibility for your own well-being

As a leader, ask yourself, whose responsibility is it to take care of you?

How many leaders do you know who take this responsibility seriously?

I have certainly met many leaders through my work who are not taking responsibility for their health and well-being.

Here is a transcript of a coaching conversation I had with Richard (not his real name). He is a partner in an accountancy firm. He's in his forties and advises large corporations.

"So, Richard, you have been analyzing your working patterns for the last couple of weeks. What have you found out?"

"Well, Sue, I am amazed at how many hours a week I am working. I have developed a habit of coming into work at 7am and not stopping until I leave at 7pm. I then go home to have dinner with my wife and children, although often the children are in bed by the time I get home. During dinner I feel distracted because I know that I still have work to finish and as soon as I can I slip away and start again, often working into the early hours of the morning. When I add all of this up I am regularly working 80 hours or more a week."

"What impact has that had, Richard?"

"Well, I have recently been diagnosed with diabetes which is something I will have to live with for the rest of my life. Also, I feel anxious and stressed a lot of the time. I also feel frustrated as I want to help people and do my best for them but find myself doing the opposite."

"I notice that you were late again for our meeting today, Richard; and I hear from your colleagues that this is a regular occurrence for internal meetings. You say that you want to do your best for other people yet the pressures you have on your time cause you to let people down. Let's think about who the people are that matter most in your life. If I asked you to draw a picture of this what would it look like?"

"Well, it is a pyramid, Sue, with my clients at the top, then my partners in the firm, then my family and then my friends."

"Where are you in this picture, Richard?"

Silence

"I am not even in the picture of my own life, Sue. That makes me feel very sad. I am embarrassed to be crying in front of you but this realization has really affected me emotionally."

"So, what is the learning you are taking from this, Richard?"

"I can't be there for other people if I don't look after myself. That seems an odd thing to say as I was always brought up to put others first but I can see now that that does not work if I don't first look after myself."

I am sure you know people who lead similar lives; maybe you are one of them. You'll be pleased to know that Richard re-created the picture of his life as a circle with himself at the center and realized that if he didn't learn to look after himself and start to create some boundaries around his work he would not be able to "be there" for all the people who mattered to him. This represented a fundamental shift in his thinking. As Arianna Huffington says, "it is about putting on your own oxygen mask first".

What benefits does being healthy bring?

Not all leaders are like Richard; I do meet other leaders who have a lifestyle that ensures they stay fit and healthy.

Isn't it true that when you are fit and healthy you handle stress better, you have more energy and you feel a greater sense of well-being?

What is interesting though is that according to research from the Centre for Creative Leadership, executives who are physically fit are considered to be more effective leaders than those who aren't. So, there is now evidence to link looking after your health with more sustainable high performance at work and enhanced leadership competence.

So, would you agree that your level of well-being and fitness not only affects your performance at work but also what happens in the rest of your life?

When I refer to health I regard it as having three key aspects:
- Brain health
- Stress management
- Healthy beliefs

I am not an expert in any of these areas but I will share with you what I have found from research and personal experience. If this flags some areas of concern for you then I suggest that you consult the appropriate experts and I'll be happy to point you in the direction of some great people. You can contact me at sue@suecoyne.com

Brain health – your competitive advantage

Is brain health something you have ever considered? I hadn't until quite recently.

Science used to think that our brain was fixed once we became an adult and that it degraded with age. In the past decade, however, our understanding of human brain capacity has fundamentally changed. Neuroscientists have discovered that our brain has neuroplasticity. Neuroplasticity refers to the lifelong capacity of the brain to change and rewire itself meaning that we can continually learn throughout life. So, brain health is about retaining the neuroplasticity of your brain.

What would you do if you walked into the CEO's office in your business and found that a seven-year-old was in charge?

Why am I asking you such an obscure question? Let me explain.

You may have the best laptop but if you have got software from 1990 how well will it perform in this day and age?

Well, most of the hardwiring in our brains, which forms the basis of our way of thinking and behaving, is in place by the time we are seven-years-old, as I have already mentioned. The problem is that we are not taught about the need to update this wiring as we go through life.

So, as a result, many of us have a seven-year-old running our lives as adults. It's a bit like updating the software on your laptop.

Isn't it true that leaders sometimes have the attitude that now they are a leader they have arrived and they have nothing to learn? What would be the impact of someone like that in your organization? What happens in companies whose leaders have stopped learning?

Think about how fast the world is changing – how do we keep pace with it if we are not learning all of the time?

On the day he was assassinated in November 1963 JF Kennedy was on his way to make a speech at the Dallas Trade Mart. If he had made the speech we would have heard him say that to his way of thinking "leadership and learning are indispensable to each other". He was a great leader. His words remind us of the need for leaders to be constantly evolving and learning and to inspire their people to do the same.

What if someone asked you whether you felt that learning was an essential part of leadership? What would you say?

Would you agree that looking after the health of your brain is important to ensure that you maintain your ability to learn?

I believe that exercising your brain is as important as exercising your body. If you continue to build what is called your cognitive reserve through mental practice and a healthy lifestyle, you are likely to maintain your brain's plasticity and your ability to learn as you age; and there is some evidence that it will reduce your likelihood of suffering from dementia or Alzheimer's disease. I am sure you know of someone who is suffering from Alzheimer's disease or dementia. If you do you will be well aware of the impact it has on their lives. Imagine what it would be like for the people you care about to have to watch you endure that disease.

Does it make sense to you that if there is something you can do to avoid this that you should start doing it?

As a leader and CEO of our own health, maintaining the neuroplasticity of your brain is part of your job.

Stress – don't let it get you down

Another key aspect of the health and well-being of a leader is being able to handle stress.

Our brain is wired to sense danger and then put us into a state of fight/flight/freeze to help us to survive the danger. Because we need all the energy to run or fight our brain shuts down our pre-frontal cortex which is the executive center where we have our short term memory and do all of our best thinking and planning. This completely disables us from operating effectively as leaders.

Also, stress hormones such as cortisol and adrenaline are released into our system. This is alright in short bursts but as many leaders are operating in a stressful state for extended periods the on-going presence of these hormones in the body can cause health problems.

Our nervous system is designed for short bursts of intense stress and the fact that we are now living at those levels of stress for much of the time results in the nervous system forgetting how to relax/release. Our muscles need to relax to allow blood flow and therefore oxygen in and toxins out. It is the same for our nervous system, which needs to be able to completely unravel and find peace and joy.

So stress can really impact our lives.

In order to enhance our ability to cope with stress we need to change our attitude. Students on my leadership programs find the tips on how to reduce stress and wire their brain for success helpful in changing their attitude towards stress and in building practices which enable them to maintain a stress-free state even when under pressure.

Breathing exercises are important when managing stress as they slow us down, connect our mind to our body and help us to be more present in the moment. This helps us to have a clearer perspective on any situation.

For many, exercise is another effective way to reduce stress. Exercise is something leaders often abandon when busy and stressed which is the very time they need to be at their most creative.

This doesn't have to be heart-pumping stuff. Get moving and exercise whenever you can. Walk instead of driving. Take the stairs.

Your beliefs can make you sick... or healthy

Did you know that the average person has 100,000 thoughts every day, a thought every second? The University of Calcutta in India found that 95 percent of our thoughts are negative and can have a stressful impact on the body.

Why do thoughts matter? Have you ever tried to change your behavior? Were you successful? Many of us try our best but never quite seem to sustain the new behavior.

What many of us don't realize is that to change our behavior we have to change our thinking. This is because our thoughts and beliefs influence our emotions, which influence our behavior. So, to change our behaviors we have to go back to our thoughts and beliefs.

What does neuroscience tell us about all of this? Scientists have discovered that we can only hold a maximum of seven concepts (plus or minus two) at a time in our working memory. So, in order to cope with the huge amount of information and thoughts the brain has to deal with it identifies those that are significant or occur frequently and "hardwires" them. It pushes them into our long-term memory, which has more capacity. Therefore, all of our habits and established beliefs are stored in our subconscious mind. What this means is that our habits are not only hardwired but they also happen without conscious thought. We wouldn't be able to walk or drive a car without this. When you first learn to drive you have to think of everything consciously, which is difficult and takes a lot of effort. As you get more practice this becomes hardwired and an unconscious competence – you can do it without thinking.

To add to this understanding from neuroscience it is worth mentioning a bit more about having a seven-year-old running our lives as adults. Up to the age of seven our mind is like a sponge and much of what is hardwired in our subconscious brains was established during this period by taking on beliefs from our parents and adult carers. What this means is that 95 percent of our behaviors as adults are being controlled by the programs in our subconscious minds that were installed when we were a child, many of which are other people's programs. Even more concerning is that 70 percent or more of these programs are negative and self-sabotaging.

When you are faced with choosing how to behave, what to say or what decision to make in relation to something that is happening externally, your brain filters the information relating to it through your existing mental models that are hardwired into your subconscious.

So, what happens is your brain filters the information coming in to find things which confirm your hardwired beliefs. These beliefs become your thoughts and your inner dialogue which influence how you feel, what you do and the outcomes you get as a result. It becomes a self-fulfilling prophecy, which is not easy to break out of.

The reason it is difficult is that your brain likes certainty; it likes to maintain the status quo and does not like change. So, you tend to hold onto your hardwired view of the world for fear that if you change it your world may collapse. What this means is that in a world that is constantly and rapidly changing your view of the world very quickly becomes out-dated and holds you back or keeps you stuck. We are not taught about the need to regularly scan our beliefs and update those that are no longer aligned with the outcomes we want. We don't realize that we need to update our software.

Learning how to do this, how to let go of beliefs that hold you back, is an important leadership skill. We call these beliefs, limiting beliefs.

So, how do you update these hardwired limiting beliefs?

You might think that one of the things you could do would be to read about new ideas. Well, unfortunately the subconscious mind is not affected by the conscious mind, so reading a book would not have any lasting impact in terms of changing the beliefs in the subconscious.

Research has shown that there are three ways to access the subconscious and start to change it:

1) Hypnosis – works at the same brainwave level as when we were absorbing our programming up to the age of seven which makes the subconscious receptive rather than resistant.
2) Repetition/practice/focus - every time you catch yourself doing an old behavior and stop yourself it reports back to the brain that you don't want this and eventually a new habit/neural pathway is formed.
3) Shock – a wake-up call which impacts your whole being.

However, the first step is to bring these limiting beliefs to conscious awareness. As they have been in place for so long they are buried deep in the subconscious and it takes patience and skill to bring them to the surface.

Some of the common limiting beliefs I have come across with the leaders I have coached include:
- I need to be perfect to be a good leader
- I need to know everything to be a good leader

- I need to be right
- I'm not good enough
- I will get found out some day (I don't deserve this position)
- I need to work hard to prove I'm good enough
- If I make a mistake, ask for help or admit I don't know others will think I can't do my job or that I am weak – and ultimately I may lose my job
- If I challenge others or express a different opinion others won't like me
- If you want something doing right it is best to do it yourself/no one can do it as well as I can
- I have to fix everything

I am sure you are well aware of the impact that some of these beliefs can have on an individual and on an organization.

Isn't it true that if you operate in a culture in which you always have to be right or perfect you are unlikely to stretch beyond your comfort zone and therefore unlikely to have enough learning and novelty in your work to keep you brain healthy?

Once you have identified your limiting beliefs you can start to identify what would be a more empowering set of new beliefs given the outcomes you want to bring about.

Neuroscience has shown us that you can't just overwrite these existing beliefs which are hardwired into neural pathways in your subconscious brain. The only way is to create new neural pathways for the new beliefs that you identify.

If you want to find out more about how to re-wire your limiting beliefs go to **https://suecoyne.com/stopdoingstartleading/**

In order to hardwire a new behavior we need to focus on it enough over time that it becomes embedded in our subconscious. There are a number of possible ways to do this which involve thinking about it, speaking about it (possibly using positive statements called affirmations) and trying out the new behavior and getting feedback.

Sometimes we all need help with this. Ideally, you would ask someone to encourage you and give you positive feedback whenever they see you doing the new behavior. Also, whilst you are in the process of hardwiring the new behavior you will lapse into the old one (albeit less and less frequently over time) and again it is good to have someone who will remind you about the new behavior so you can focus your attention on it again.

Learning to more consciously choose your thoughts and behavior is important as a leader as you have an impact on those around you. 70 percent of what happens in an organization comes from imitating the leaders.

Are you over-focusing on your work and making health and well-being a poor second in terms of priority, or are you taking responsibility for looking after your health and well-being and making it a priority?

The thing I would like you to remember is this: It is better to put effort into maintaining good health than to take it for granted until the day it is taken away from you.

Reflection space

Where does health fit into your definition of success?

How would you rate yourself out of 10 (where 10 is the best score) for health and well-being?

What insights have you got from this chapter that you would like to try out?

Chapter 8
Being a Happy Leader

"Happiness is an attitude. We either make ourselves miserable or happy and strong. The amount of work is the same." Francesca Reigler

Happy leaders are effective leaders

How do you perform when you are not happy? Do you feel at your most effective?

How about when you are happy? Isn't it great to feel that joie de vivre that happiness brings so that you look forward to each day and enjoy your life and your work?

What makes you happy?

Is it something you find on the outside?

Many people have a tendency to believe that when we lose weight, earn more money or have the car/house/partner we are dreaming of we will be happy. For many of those people, when you get whatever it is, the happiness is short lived.

This is illustrated by the fact that personal incomes more than doubled between 1960 and the late 1990s but the proportion of people who described themselves as happy remained stable at 30 percent. It seems that once you are above the poverty line more money contributes less and less to your happiness.

Many people think that if they work harder they will be more successful and they'll be happier. Have you ever been so busy striving to achieve a goal that you got addicted to the destination and forgot to enjoy the journey?

What people tend to do is change the goalposts of what success looks like every time they have some success. Success is a moving target. The minute you achieve something you start trying to achieve the next thing. So happiness is indefinitely postponed.

Happiness is not about what is happening in the external world – only 10 percent of our long-term happiness is external. 90 percent is how we process that external world.

So, if striving for external things and achieving our goals does not give us lasting happiness, what does?

Can it come from serving others?

Happiness research confirms that true happiness makes us naturally want to serve others. It motivates us to be generous and to use our success to support other people's success as well.

Albert Schweitzer spent his life working for a more just, peaceful and sustainable world. He said, "The only ones among you who will be really happy are those who have sought and found how to serve."

Here's a story that makes this point:

- Once a group of 500 people were attending a seminar. Suddenly the speaker stopped and decided to do a group activity. He started giving each person a balloon. Each person was then asked to write their name on it using a marker pen. Then all the balloons were collected and put in another room.
- The people were then let into that room and asked to find the balloon which had their name written on it within five minutes. Everyone was frantically searching for their name, colliding with each other, pushing around others and there was utter chaos.
- At the end of five minutes no one could find their own balloon. Then, the speaker asked each person to randomly collect a balloon and give it to the person whose name was written on it. Within minutes everyone had their own balloon.
- The speaker then began, "This is happening in our lives. Everyone is frantically looking for happiness all around, not knowing where it is."
- Our happiness lies in the happiness of other people. Give them their happiness and you will get your own happiness.

Doing something to make other people happy doesn't have to take a lot of time or effort. Why not try the following:

For three days in a row when you wake up in the morning write two emails/text messages praising or thanking someone.

Your brain thinks you are amazing for doing this and you get great emails back. When people do this their sense of social connection escalates. The reason why this is so important is that social connection is not only the greatest predictor of long-term happiness but also a predictor of how long we will live.

Is happiness something innate?

I believe that happiness is something we have on the inside, not something we need to look for on the outside.

Have you ever been in the company of someone who is genuinely happy and found that happiness to be infectious? Inner happiness radiates out and affects those around you and makes them want to spend time in your presence.

The Ancient Greeks defined happiness as the *joy* of moving towards our potential. When you think about happiness not just as pleasure but as a joy that moves us towards our potential you get a very different picture of the connection between happiness and success. This inner joy enhances your performance at work, attracts positive relationships, generates a feeling of satisfaction with life and helps you to be healthier and live longer. Yes, there has actually been research that has proven that happier people live 14 percent longer than miserable people, increasing longevity by 7.5 to 10 years.

How can you create a feeling of inner happiness?

Take a few minutes to think of a really happy moment that you have experienced and stay with it until you feel a big smile break out on your face. Notice how that makes you feel on the inside.

Let's have a look at how that affects your brain chemistry. There are two happiness chemicals in the brain – dopamine and oxytocin. Many studies suggest that as we age we are constantly losing our stores of dopamine, which is why we need to seek out experiences that release dopamine. The two best ways to increase your brain's dopamine production are smiling and exercise.

What are you doing to replenish your levels of dopamine?

What about oxytocin? How can we increase oxytocin levels in the brain?

Some of you may not like this! It involves hugging or being hugged by others (a minimum of eight times a day}. Imagine that in the workplace! Other ways to increase levels of oxytocin include stroking pets, having a massage, watching romantic films, dancing, meditating and making music, particularly in the company of others. Believe it or not, it also includes using Twitter and Facebook.

What do you do that increases your levels of oxytocin?

Does *your* brain have the chemistry of happiness?

A study done by Richard Davidson, a professor of psychology and psychiatry at the University of Wisconsin, showed that when Buddhist Monks experienced bliss as they entered into a trance-like state when deep in meditation, the left prefrontal lobe of their brain (above the left eyebrow) showed increased electrical activity. The findings in this study suggested that bliss or happiness is not just a vague feeling, but a physical state of the brain.

More importantly, this physical state can be induced deliberately. He refers to this as making a left shift.

Here are some ways that you can make a left shift and cultivate happiness:

- Yoga and Chi Gung
- Exercise – 20-30 minutes of fast exercise four or five days a week
- Walks with your dog
- Meditate for 20 minutes, three times a week for three weeks
- Create noise-cancelling moments as suggested by Shawn Achor in *The Happiness Advantage*[9]:

- For two minutes a day take your hands off the keyboard and do nothing, just watch your breath going in and out. This simple action causes your brain to have a moment of quiet.

- Stop looking at emails after 5pm; have an hour on Sunday with no electronics; spend the first five minutes in the car with the radio off.

These noise-cancelling moments allow our brains to retrieve the resources they need in order to scan the world for why we could feel happy in that present moment. If you can decrease the amount of noise in your brain by just 5 percent your brain can focus on what it means to *be* human as opposed to focusing so much on what you are doing. There is a place in all of us where we can experience inner happiness and peace; we just have to access it.

"Those who can sit in a chair, undistracted for hours, mastering subjects and creating things will rule the world, while the rest of us frantically and futilely try to keep up with texts, tweets and other incessant interruptions." - Eric Baker

Another way to cultivate happiness is to focus on gratitude. Gratitude connects you with your own strength, peace and wisdom. Here are two ways to practice gratitude:

- Generate a sense of gratitude by asking yourself: What am I grateful for? What do I feel blessed about that is ahead of me today? What do I appreciate about what happened today?
- Start a gratitude list that you share with others every day

What has happiness got to do with going from doing to leading?

The evidence shows that companies with higher than average employee happiness have better financial performance and customer satisfaction.

70 percent of what happens in an organization comes from imitating the leaders, as I have already mentioned. Cultures that create stress and burnout also create unhappiness. As a leader it is your job to create a positive work environment and contribute to the happiness of your people. Research has shown that happiness brings out the best in people. So, why not start to cultivate an environment which creates happiness?

This starts with you developing a happiness mind-set.

Are you driven only by profitability and productivity? Do you see happiness as something for outside of work?

What makes a happy mind-set is the belief that creating happiness for yourself is not self-indulgent but a necessity as it is a performance enhancer, for you and those around you. If you choose happiness in the moment everything we can test for improves – intelligence, creativity and productivity. Then you find your success rates rise and you can share that happiness. Happiness creates competitive advantage.

You can create happiness in those around you by showing people that you care and are there to serve them. Who could you surprise today with some extra attention? What could you do to appreciate someone today?

What is your level of happiness?

Are you still striving to find that one thing that will make you happy? Or are you creating an inner attitude of positive enthusiasm which makes you attractive to others, makes you want to share your happiness with others and generates the sort of success that breeds a deep satisfaction in your life?

The thing I would like you to remember is this:
"Success is not the key to happiness, happiness is the key to success."
- Albert Schweitzer

Reflection space

What is your definition of happiness?

Why does being a happy leader matter?

How would you rate yourself out of 10 (where 10 is the best score) for your current level of happiness?

What insights have you got from this chapter that you want to try out?

STAGE THREE – EFFECTIVE EMPOWERMENT

Chapter 9
Empowering Yourself and Others

"As we look ahead into the next century leaders will be those who empower others." - Bill Gates

The intention in this chapter is to share with you how the thinking around empowerment has evolved including the latest neuroscience that underpins it. Then to give you an understanding of how to empower people in a way that works for both you and them and delivers the desired outcomes.

Why does empowerment matter?

For you to be able to step up into your leadership role it is crucial to learn to let go of control and empower your people to do what they need to be doing and so free up the time you need in order to lead. Once you start to trust and empower others effectively they will be energized and you will feed off that energy and be energized yourself. They will be like your battery charger.

So, what difference would it make to everyone's effectiveness if you created an environment of trust and empowerment?

What is true empowerment?

Literally, empowerment involves managers and leaders sharing some of their power and giving up some of their control. Giving up control is something that many leaders find difficult.

Think about the last time you felt empowered. What contributed to you feeling empowered? What was the experience like?

How does that compare to times when you have been disempowered (had your freedom to act taken away), or when you were not empowered (had not been given the freedom to act in the first place)?

A definition of empowerment is:

Enabling individuals and teams to translate the organization's strategic goals into their day-to-day goals and letting them get on with executing them. Your job is to create the conditions for empowerment and then become a source of help and support as required.

It is a win-win situation as it means that people can do the work in a way that is right for them whilst at the same time meeting the organization's needs of them. To make this possible you need to agree on the outcomes and provide clear boundaries within which people are empowered.

When you empower someone they take on the accountability and responsibility for the results.

How does it differ from delegation?

Delegation involves a similar process to empowerment, but here parts of your own job are given away to someone else. You pass on the responsibility but the accountability stays with you.

Freda's been experimenting with empowerment but she's not at all convinced about the idea. First, there was the global protocol alignment project. Freda had wanted to take on the task herself, having been responsible in her former lead scientist role for the original UK protocols. She very much doubted anyone else would be able to do the job properly. But Tony, the MD, had said her time would be better spent working on the departmental restructure and had asked Freda to empower Sarah, her replacement as lead scientist.

Though she'd had serious doubts, Freda had seen she had little choice but to agree. But she was determined to keep a close eye on the project. It was too risky to simply let Sarah get on with it. So she'd explained in great detail how she'd gone about the original UK project, and told her she expected to see her work in the same way across the wider company. She'd also asked Sarah to run any problems past her and check with her before making any significant decisions. That was turning out to be a very wise move, she reflected. Sarah's approach in some areas was turning out to be very different from her own, and she was having to put her foot down quite firmly. The trouble was that Sarah seemed to have lost all enthusiasm for the project, which was strange. She'd been really keen at first.

Then there was Rob. Rob had joined the department bringing solid experience from their main competitor, Bio Molds. He'd proved extremely competent in his new role and she'd quickly given him extra responsibilities. He'd accepted willingly, saying he was looking forward to the challenge. He'd seemed so confident, Freda hadn't felt the need to schedule in regular catch-ups and she hadn't seen much of him at all in the last few weeks. Rob had emailed her a couple of times but she'd been too busy to get back to him. She had far too much on her plate and she'd assumed he'd manage. But she was hearing rumors he was struggling, and she had to admit the figures in his first report were looking decidedly odd.

On top of that, Lisa in LA had called her, worried that Rob didn't seem to understand what he was doing. Freda supposed she would have to talk to him. She sighed. Her colleague, Effective Ellie, had told her empowerment would help increase motivation, bring about new ideas and allow others to take on accountability. She wasn't seeing any of that. Instead, empowerment was turning out to be just one headache after another.

How empowerment increases brain power

The first time I learnt about delegation and empowerment was in the context of **Situational Leadership.** This model was developed by Hersey and Blanchard in the late 1970s/early 1980s. Their premise was that there is no "best" style of leadership and successful leaders adapt their style according to the confidence and capability of the person relative to the task involved. This is an aspect of leadership style agility that we will discuss in the bonus chapter on the core capabilities of empowerment.

I feel that this is a bit out-dated now but the premise still holds true that the leader needs to adjust their involvement in the task according to the level of competence and confidence of the other person in relation to that particular task.

When I learnt about empowerment and delegation it was in the 1990s and I didn't quite grasp the situational aspect to it. I had a Senior Research Executive reporting to me. She was very capable in all aspects of that role and I was able to really empower her. I promoted her to Associate Director and was surprised when she began to struggle. I soon realized that I needed to come in closer and give her more support on the aspects of the role that were new to her. She needed some coaching to build her confidence and develop her ability in those areas.

The situational leadership model is a bit out-dated because what we have learnt from **neuroscience** since the early 2000s has moved this thinking on. It highlights the need for empowerment and delegation to be supported by coaching.

The key principles from neuroscience that are relevant to this are as follows:

Everyone's brain is different

Our brains have around 100 billion neurons. The connections between our neurons are the maps that guide our thoughts, behaviors and actions. We have more than 300 trillion of these constantly-changing connections. So, there are unlimited ways that our brains can store information.

This means that everyone's brain is different.

Our environment shapes the physical nature of our brains. Therefore, our brains were already quite different to each other's at birth. Since then, the circuitry of our brain has been molded by every sound, thought, feeling, idea and experience for our whole lives. The way we store, organize, manage and retrieve information is as different between two people as two laptops would be after 40 years of use.

Why does this matter?

How often have you assumed that the way you do a task is the best way and advised someone else to do it the same way? What are the chances of that being right for their brain given that every brain is different?

Doing the thinking for other people is not just a waste of our own energy, it also gets in the way of them working out the right answers and doing things in a way that works for their brain.

Have you ever had one of those *aha* moments when you got a new insight? How did you feel after that insight? The chances are you felt energized to act on it. Enabling others to have their own insights will ensure they are doing what is right for their brain and are energized. Encouraging them to take action when they feel energized will ensure they make progress.

Creating a positive environment helps performance

This is fundamental to effective empowerment. The brain has an overarching organizing principle, which is to classify the world around you into things that will either hurt you or help you stay alive – this is about minimizing danger or maximizing reward.

There are two possible states that result from this. The *away* state, which is about threat or danger. In this state we move into fight/flight/freeze mode. The adrenaline is up and we are ready to move quickly. The pre-frontal cortex which is the working memory is shut down to conserve energy so you are unable to think clearly and make good decisions. The *toward* state involves an increase in dopamine and endorphins. In this state you are engaged, solution-focused and can take a global view. People in this state are more creative and can think clearly.

It is important to remember that when you are empowering or delegating to people they will be more receptive and able to do their own thinking around it if they are in the *toward* state.

What can you do to ensure they are in a *toward* state? I have often shared the S.A.F.E.R. model with leaders to help them to work out how to encourage a reward state.

S.A.F.E.R. relates to the five social domains of the brain: security, autonomy, fairness, ego and relatedness. We all have our own hierarchy in terms of how important these things are to us. Here are some suggestions of how to create a *toward* state for each one in turn:

Security – being clear about your expectations, the timescale and the required outcomes
Autonomy – giving people a choice or letting them have a say in things which affect them
Fairness – being treated fairly and in the same way as others
Ego – focusing on strengths; focusing attention completely on the person; not acting as if you are the expert; not sitting behind a desk
Relatedness – building trust, a sense of community and belonging

What would be the impact if you were to create a reward state using S.A.F.E.R. for the people you want to empower? Creating a reward state using S.A.F.E.R. increases engagement, motivation and performance and is useful not only when empowering others but in any situation where there is a risk that people will feel threatened and go into an away state. It is particularly useful when leading change.

Learning something new uses more energy

When we learn something new it rearranges the way our brain works. We have to build new neural pathways. This is done by creating connections between the synapses. The first time a signal passes from one brain cell to another it is like crossing a deep ravine and it takes a lot of effort and energy. That is why learning something new is difficult to start with. As the signal passes between the two cells again and again it builds a more solid pathway. Then it becomes effortless and we can do it whenever we like.

Sometimes it feels monumental to do something new, to take the first step. Helping people to have insights themselves and see things differently involves them taking that initial leap and this creates fear. They need your encouragement and support at that stage. Positive feedback will encourage them to repeat and hardwire the new behavior.

To sum up these four principles from neuroscience:

- Everyone's brain is different so telling them how to do something is a waste of your energy and theirs as the chances are even though it is right for your brain it is most likely not right for theirs
- Supporting people to do their own thinking and have their own insights energizes and motivates them
- Your role as leader is to create a *toward* state where people are engaged and solution focused. You can use S.A.F.E.R. to do this.
- Once they have come up with their solution you can encourage them to follow through with it by giving positive feedback and keeping their attention focused on it

What does this mean in terms of your role in helping others to succeed?

The role of a leader is to set up the conditions of empowerment and then get out of the way and become a source of help as required. It is not about getting your ego stroked but getting the job done.

How you can make it happen

I like to build on strengths when I am coaching. Often my clients are very task focused and are good at managing projects, so I ask them, "If empowering people was a project, what would you do?"

If I asked you that question what would you come up with? They usually come up with a similar process to the one I will describe to you.

Step One: Preparation

Climate

What creates the sort of environment in which people feel psychologically safe to get out of their comfort zones and learn new things?

What makes it safe for people to make mistakes and learn from them?

What makes them feel able to ask for help?

If you are challenging them to get out of their comfort zone they need to know that the support is there when they need it. Otherwise, you will create stress and anxiety and put them into an *away* state, creating a burnout culture. However, research has shown that high support that is not balanced with sufficient challenge becomes too chilled out and does not result in high performance.

Challenge/Support Matrix

	Low SUPPORT	High SUPPORT
High **CHALLENGE**	**Burnout culture** • On-going Stress • Anxious energy • Adversarial • Unsustainable results	**High performance culture** • High motivation • High energy • Meritocracy • Fail fast/allow mistakes • Sustainable results
Low	**Comfort Zone culture** • Boredom and depression • Low energy • Minimal effort • No results	**Peace and harmony culture** • Avoidance energy • No conflicts, nice guys • Anything goes • Results don't matter

Low SUPPORT High

Think of a leader for whom you have worked and who had a significant impact on you and your development. What did they do that enabled them to have such an impact? What people often say to me when I ask this question is that the leader believed in them more than they believed in themselves.

What happens when someone does this? The other person steps up to the plate to repay that belief in them. This is about using behaviors that affirm the other person and also about challenging them to stretch themselves, not so far that it creates fear but far enough to stimulate and motivate.

When they know you are there to provide support if and when they need it they will be willing to grow and learn from their mistakes and failures. So, creating the right climate is part of the preparation.

Mind-set

The next step in your preparation is to manage your mindset.

Why does this matter? Remember that how you think influences how you feel which influences your behavior. Also in the bonus chapter on the Core Capabilities of Empowerment you will learn about mirror neurons and emotions being contagious. When preparing to empower it is good to start with asking yourself the question, *Why?*

Use this to create a compelling reason *why* it is important to empower your people and to do it effectively. How does it benefit the organization? How does it benefit the team? How does it benefit you and the person being empowered? Then move on to making sure you have beliefs that are aligned with what you want to achieve.

What are your beliefs about getting things done? Here are some of the beliefs my clients have had over the years:

- *There is only one way to do things – my way.*
- *If you want to get something done well it is better to do it yourself.*

- *It is my job as leader to take on all the responsibility and fix things for my people.*

OR

- *It is my job to develop my people, to enable them to grow and realize their potential and allow me to realize mine.*

What are one or two beliefs that will underpin you successfully empowering your people?

How you see people is how they show up

If you see people as incapable or not good enough they will pick up on that and it will undermine their confidence and their willingness to take on additional responsibility.

Before meeting with someone to talk about empowering them, make sure that you clear any assumptions, preconceptions, judgments or negative views about them.

Instead think of all of the potential and possibilities they have as they realize this potential with your support.

What would be the impact on you if you shifted to this sort of mind-set? And what would be the impact on your people?

When preparing for empowerment it is always useful to ask yourself the question – what does success look like?

The final step in terms of preparation is to focus on your behavior. Ask yourself these questions:

- *How* can I model trustworthiness and build trust?
- *How* can I make sure they feel accepted and valued for who they are, not just for what they do, and that what they are doing matters?
- *What* emotions do I want them to pick up from me?
- *How* can I show empathy and that I understand their perspective?
- *How* can I use S.A.F.E.R. to support myself and the person I am empowering?
- *How* do I want the other person to feel at the end of the first meeting? How do I want them to feel at the end of the whole process?
- *How* do I need to behave to achieve this?

What difference would it make to the effectiveness of your empowerment process if you took the time to do this sort of preparation? There are differing views on preparation and its contribution to success but one thing is for sure: when you are developing a new skill it is an essential part of the process.

Step Two: Optimising the process

The purpose of this step is to ensure that both you and the person being empowered are clear on the steps involved and that the process works for both of you.

This is part of an initial set-up meeting that you have with the person you are empowering. The idea is that you co-design the empowerment process – in other words, you both put your needs on the table and design a process that meets both sets of needs.

What do you need to do to ensure the meeting is set up in the most appropriate way?

- Agree a suitable time and place for this, making sure you allow sufficient time
- Agree on an agenda with the person and what would make the meeting a success for both of you
- Treat the meeting as a conversation and encourage the person being empowered to ask questions to get the level of clarification they need to move forward (different people need different levels of clarification before they are happy to take the first steps)

The questions you might want to discuss in the meeting are:
- What are the desired outcomes and timings?

- What does the other person believe are their strengths in relation to this task?
- For which aspects of the task do they feel they will need support?
- What level of input would they like from you?
- What are your needs from the process (you might need an update for a meeting on a specific date or just to give you confidence that it is going to plan)?
- What inputs will they need from others?
- What would a mutually agreeable empowerment process and timeline look like?

Step Three: Creating win-win

Step three means creating an empowerment process that perpetuates a *toward* environment. Without this there is a risk that people will feel they are doing all the giving and getting nothing back.

How can you ensure that the empowerment process is a win-win for all concerned?

This might be part of the same initial meeting or a separate one.

- Set the expectation that what you would like to end up with is a win-win agreement which is mutually beneficial for you both
- How does this opportunity fit with their learning and development objectives?

- How does it fit with the other things they are doing both in terms of workload and prioritization and also in terms of content?
- What could you make this meaningful and valuable for them?
- How can this be achieved at the same time as delivering the desired outcomes from the team/company perspective?
- Make sure you leave the meeting with clearly defined expectations in terms of outcomes and timing that you both agree and understand
- Make sure responsibilities and accountability are clear as are any boundaries/parameters

How good are you at holding people accountable, including yourself? Leaders often struggle with this. In fact, Harris Interactive in the US found that only 10 percent of people feel that their company holds them accountable for results.

What impact does this lack of accountability have?

People I coach regularly complain that at every meeting deadlines slip and there are no consequences. Often the leader is all too aware that everyone has a heavy workload and lets them off the hook. If someone consistently fails to deliver and is under performing it is really important to be seen to address this, otherwise those who are performing can become demotivated.

What does the employee require so that they are willing to be held accountable?

- Understanding needs – they need to understand what needs to be done and be given clear outcomes and expectations.
- Authority – they need to be empowered to do it
- Ownership – they need to be committed to doing it
- Mutual accountability – everyone including you needs to be held accountable for delivering on their commitments. Mutual accountability is vital as employees can't deliver without you and you can't deliver without them; hence, this being a key part in creating a win-win empowerment environment. Part and parcel of making mutual accountability work is being able to have courageous conversations with the team members who fail to deliver.

Remember:

You can't manage outcomes without accountability and all good people want to be held accountable. So, it needs to be part of every relationship you have with your people.

Step Four: Enabling

This is about you **enabling** the person you are empowering.

How do you enable them right from the first meeting? You could explain that they are free to deliver the outcomes in whatever way works for them. Ask if they would like some support in starting to think about how to go about this. You could use S.A.F.E.R. to frame this discussion:

Security – explain the expectations, timescale and outcomes. Agree on them and ask them to play them back so it is clear that they have the same understanding as you. Agree milestones/review meetings along the way.

Autonomy – ask open questions to help them do their own thinking. What? How? When? Where? How do you plan to go about this? What first steps are you going to take? How confident/energized do you feel to take the first steps in a score out of 10? What would help to increase that score?

Fairness – What would make you feel that this is a fair process? Agree on no judgment or criticism as part of that.

Ego – what are your strengths in relation to this? How can you build on them?

Relatedness – what support do you need from me or from colleagues?

And of course, listen.

What else is involved in your role as an enabler after the first empowerment set-up meeting?

Your role as enabler includes:

- Removing any barriers that get in the way of delivering the outcomes
- Providing help and support as required
- Providing encouragement and positive feedback informally
- Supporting with coaching to help the person identify how to overcome setbacks etc.
- Making sure the agreed review meetings take place and helping the person assess whether they are on track by asking questions and providing feedback. Support them in adjusting if they are not on track (we are all off track most of the time and need feedback to realign ourselves to ensure we arrive at our agreed destination). Encourage a positive mindset even if they do go off track by helping them to focus on what has gone well and how they can build on it.

Step Five: Review and recognition

How do you normally end a project? How do you evaluate how it has gone?

This is no different. You end with review and recognition.

You could convene a final review meeting in which you have a conversation about how it went and how you both feel about the process and the outcomes.

Key aspects of this conversation are:
- Reviewing the process
- Reviewing against the agreed outcomes
- Celebrating what went well – making sure you ask them what they would like to celebrate
- Giving recognition
- Celebrating the results and encouraging them to build on them in the future
- Sharing what you have both learnt from this process

So, there you have the five steps to effective empowerment that will energize you and your team. Enjoy experimenting with what you have learnt (you won't get it right first time, it will take practice) and develop your own approach to empowerment. Putting effort into becoming even more effective at empowering your people will mean that both you and they make a greater contribution to the success of your organization by delivering sustainable high performances.

There are four Core Capabilities that underpin your ability to be effective at empowerment: trust, rapport, emotional intelligence and style agility. I have written a bonus chapter on these four capabilities which you can download at **https://suecoyne.com/ stopdoing startleading/**

Reflection space

How would you currently rate yourself in terms of your effectiveness at empowering others (Score out of 10 where 10 is the best score)?

In six months' time what score would you like to be able to give yourself for your effectiveness at empowering others?

Why does this matter to you?

What insights have you got from this chapter that you would like to try out?

STAGE FOUR – DEVELOPING OTHERS

Chapter 10
Developing the Potential of Your People

"A good leader is one who can tell another how to reach his or her potential; a great leader is one who can help another discover this potential for him or herself." - Bo Bennett

My intention in this chapter is to help you to grow your abilities in developing the potential of others, a key part of being an inspirational leader.

Developing others allows you to Stop Doing and Start Leading

I recently read an article in *Harvard Business Review* by Monique Valcour entitled:

"If You're Not Helping People Develop, You're Not Management Material"

What do you think about that statement?

What are some of the trends in the workplace that might lend support to that view?

In the past, people joined an organization expecting a "career for life". That is no longer what is on offer. So, what they are looking for is a sustainable career. As a result, when they are deciding whether an organization is a suitable employer they want to make sure there are good opportunities for learning and development.

If you think back to how you have learnt over the years, where would you say that most of your learning has happened?

The answer I tend to get is "on the job". Sometimes as much as 90 percent of learning is on the job. Therefore, potential employees want to be sure that they will be reporting to a leader who they respect and can learn from.

Why do leaders need to develop others to add value to their organization?

Firstly, to help attract talent.

It also plays a key part in engaging and retaining talent.

A leader who develops others helps people to perform well on a sustainable basis and make the biggest contribution they can to the organization.

We talk in the bonus chapter on the Core Capabilities of Empowerment about the importance of building trust and rapport to create a climate in which people are willing to be empowered and willing to learn. When leaders take the time to develop others this helps to build trust and rapport. It also helps to create a learning culture which means that the growth in people's capabilities keeps up with the changing needs of the organization enabling it to have sustainable success.

Growing new leaders is your key to becoming a great leader

I have worked in many organizations that have grown rapidly and not invested in the growth of their leaders. Eventually they get to a situation where there is a capability gap – the leaders no longer have the capabilities to meet the organization's needs of them. This also applies to developing the people reporting to the leaders. If they are not growing they are not able to step up and take on more responsibility, which means their leaders do not have the space to grow.

If as leaders we do not develop our people **we** become a drain on the organization's potential. It means that we have a higher-than-necessary staff turnover, which has significant cost implications. It also means that our people don't contribute as much as they could which limits the organization's growth and success.

What's getting in the way?

Maybe as I said at the start you are already working long hours and don't have the time
Possibly you don't see it as part of your role
It could be that you just don't know how to do this
Or that you feel you don't have the budget to pay for it
Maybe you believe that people should take charge of their own development

Perhaps you don't have direct reports
Maybe you are a potential leader and don't yet have anyone to develop

What I am going to share with you in this chapter will support you in growing your ability to develop others whenever and wherever the opportunity arises.

As you read through this chapter reflect on whether developing others is high enough on your list of priorities.

Part of this is about becoming clear on what your role is as a leader and where developing people fits into this. David Whyte, poet and philosopher, puts it quite simply: "being an effective leader is about having effective conversations."

What makes an effective conversation from a leadership perspective? Many leaders may think it is all about performance. And yes performance is key. However, really effective conversations that lead to sustainable performance also help people to grow.

What is *your* mind-set in relation to developing your people? Is your focus a short term one? For example, I want to make sure people perform and deliver the agreed outcomes. Or do you also have an eye on the longer term? For example, I want to make sure they perform and help them to grow at the same time.

Freda has just come out of a meeting with Tony, the MD. He'd wanted to know what she was doing about developing her team. She hadn't known what to say. With her energy focused on getting people to meet the stretch performance targets she'd been given for the team, staff development hadn't exactly been a top priority. As she walked along the corridor, Freda pondered what sort of development opportunities her staff might want. In her efforts to keep operations on track and avoid delays and mistakes, she was always giving her scientists and technicians advice and answering their questions. Surely they would be learning plenty from what she was telling them?

People did still mess up sometimes, of course. And it was her job to make sure they knew what they had done wrong so that they wouldn't do it again. That was all part of their professional development; such as when Ian's latest bright idea had cost them a day's production. Afterwards, Ian had tried to tell her about what he'd learnt and asked if he could run his ideas for further research past her. She had been too worried about the immediate problem to listen and she'd simply told him not to take things any further. However, afterwards she wondered whether she'd been too harsh.

Freda's colleague, Effective Ellie, had said that it's OK to fail sometimes, as long as you used what you learnt towards the next steps. And, Freda reflected, perhaps Ian really was onto something that would help with her long-term objective of ramping up production without increasing costs. Maybe she should talk to him again, look at how she could help him perfect the techniques he was working on. Deciding to act sooner rather than later, Freda called Ian to ask if he could spare her a few minutes. He agreed and joined her in the third floor meeting room. But, before Freda had time to say anything, Ian handed her a brown envelope. "I'd hoped working here would give me lots of opportunities to learn new skills," he said. "It hasn't. I've been offered a job at Bio Molds and I've taken it."

How can you support and develop your people?

In the bonus chapter on the Core Capabilities of Empowerment you learn about six different styles of leadership. In terms of developing people, the style that is the most appropriate is the coaching style. We also learnt in the chapter on empowerment that a high-performance culture is created through a balance between challenge and support. Coaching is both challenging and supportive.

There is a lot of data that shows how effective the coaching style is. Google's people analytics team examined data from thousands of employee surveys and performance reviews to find out which behaviors characterize its most effective managers. **<u>Coaching</u>** topped the list, which also included helping with career development.

Coaching is just one aspect of having a coaching style of leadership. So, what do we mean when we talk about a coaching style?

Maybe we should start with what we don't mean. It is not about giving orders, it is not about dispensing knowledge and it is not tell-and-sell.

It involves:
Asking questions, listening and enabling others to get their own insights and find their own solutions. It takes time to perfect this style but it is worth it as it has such a positive impact.

So, if there is a repertoire of six leadership styles, when do you use the coaching style? You learn to assess the situation and select the most appropriate style in the moment. If your organization has a learning culture the chances are that the coaching style will just be part of the way you do things.

What benefits does using a coaching style bring?

It brings **you** insights as well as the person being coached. You get a better understanding of how people feel about work, their career and the organization. As we have already said it helps people to perform and learn something in the process. It helps you to anticipate performance issues before they arise. It enhances engagement as it makes the relationship between you more collaborative. When people are engaged and supported in this way they are willing to go the extra mile and as such it helps you achieve more with fewer resources. It helps your people to be clear on their strengths and development areas and supports them in developing their abilities and experimenting with new ways of doing things.

What sort of issues can you address using the coaching style?

A coaching style can be used for developing specific skills and abilities, dealing with challenges and problems, managing stress, managing relationships and changing unhelpful behavior; the key though is that it enables the people you are coaching to find their own insights and solutions to all of these issues.

The four key ways to use a coaching style

The four key ways are a combination of formal or informal situations and overt or tacit coaching. Let's have a look at each of these.

Four Different Aspects of the Coaching Style

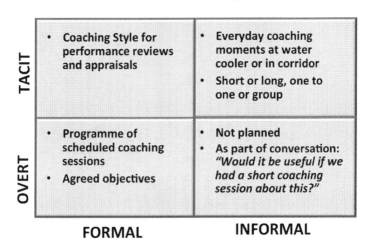

When coaching is tacit it is used as a style of having a conversation. So, at the more formal end of the spectrum, you might conduct an annual review or appraisal meeting using a coaching style.

At the informal end of that spectrum, you could have a coaching style conversation at the water cooler or coffee machine or in the corridor between meetings.

I was coaching the management team of a private equity firm recently and ran a master class for them on developing their people. They had the classic reason as to why they don't give feedback to their people

– no time! When I asked them how they could build this into their way of working they said that on the way back from meetings they could have informal developmental conversations with people. Great!

When coaching is overt and formal this would take the form of a program of pre-scheduled coaching sessions with agreed objectives. These might be conducted by you as a manager-coach, you or someone else as an internal coach or by an external professional coach.

At the informal end of the overt coaching spectrum, you might be having a conversation with someone when an issue comes up. In the moment, you ask whether a short coaching session would help to find a solution to this issue. You then switch to the coaching mode for this part of the conversation.

Hopefully, this has helped to clarify what the coaching style is and where it fits.

It is one of six possible styles that you will use in conversations with people selected according to the requirements of the situation.

When you get adept at using it you can switch in and out of it in the same conversation. It becomes part of your personal communication style. Using the coaching style does not have a beginning and an end in the way that a formal coaching session does. It is on-going.

It is about the way you have all sorts of conversations. It can be used in the delegation and empowerment process. It can be used for giving feedback and even for having difficult conversations.

What helps the coaching style to be successful?

As a professional coach, I like to work with anyone who wants to grow and develop. It helps when they understand how coaching can help them grow as this ensures they are "up" for the coaching. They want to be coached and are willing to take responsibility for acting on the insights they get from the coaching. Otherwise, it is a waste of everyone's time and energy. The same applies to your use of the coaching style.

What can stop it being successful?

A number of things come up here. If the people you are coaching don't want to change or are resistant to learning it will probably not be effective. You can also stop it being successful if you don't take the time to develop your skills in this area. It could also be hindered by the culture in the organization – if there is a strong bottom line focus and the organization doesn't yet appreciate how coaching contributes to bottom line results then the conditions are unlikely to be conducive to effective coaching.

Students on my coaching training programs learn the six steps to being effective at explicit formal coaching.

Step One – Create the right environment

The first step is to create the right **environment** for coaching.

You create the environment through your leadership style. We have already talked quite a lot in previous chapters about creating a positive reward or toward environment. It is also important to do this for coaching.

Step Two – Apply the neuroscience

We heard about the neuroscience in relation to empowerment. It is also very relevant to using the coaching style.

The key elements of neuroscience that are relevant to coaching are:
- Coaching helps people to get their own insights and be energized to act on them.
- Coaching helps to stretch people so that their brain has to try new ways of thinking and doing things.

Our brain has plasticity and we can create new neural pathways which enable us to change our behavior. Coaching supports re-wiring by encouraging progress and also by providing reminders to keep our attention focused on what we want to change.

So, neuroscience explains why the coaching style of leadership is effective.

It allows you to:
Stop giving advice and help people to think for themselves. As you do this you enable them to have their own insights, to come up with their own solutions and to identify how they need to change their behavior to bring those solutions into reality.

Just the fact that you take the time to coach them gives them support and the belief that they can develop the new habits they have identified.

How does it make you feel as a coach to see people developing and growing in this way? How does it make them feel?

The bottom line is that using a coaching style of leadership energizes everyone involved!

Step Three – Reflection

Prior to starting a formal coaching session it is important to do some reflection about:

- Where the coaching should take place
- How to create a safe space in which you can have an open and honest conversation
- How to create a pull rather than a push style, moving from being a solution provider to a solution enabler

Step Four – Effective coaching process

What does an effective coaching process looks like? It starts with contracting and then includes having a clear process to guide your coaching conversations.

How do you establish a coaching contract?

As external coaches, we establish a very clear contract with our coachees.

What should and could be in a coaching contract between an internal coach and their coachee?

There are some easy answers – logistics about the coaching program, expectations of each other, objectives for the coaching and for the session.

It is worth reflecting on and discussing with the coachee what else needs to be in your contract to ensure the coaching is as effective as possible.

There are some issues that are less obvious – one of them is confidentiality.

As external coaches we offer 100 percent confidentiality.

What level of confidentiality is it appropriate for you to offer as a manager-coach or an internal coach?

What process should you follow?

Another requirement of effective coaching is having a process that ensures that the coaching conversation is a productive one.

There are a number of coaching models or frameworks available to help with this. The best-known one is probably the GROW model developed by Sir John Whitmore. Another popular one is CIGAR developed by Full Potential Group.

In my online program both are explained in detail with example questions and guidance about putting them into practice.

The coaching conversation will not always follow the order of the model but it gives you a framework that you can hold in your mind and keep coming back to.

Step Five – Develop your coaching skills

Coaching involves moving from push to pull. Traditionally coaching is non-directive. You listen and reflect back by paraphrasing and summarizing to show you understand. You ask powerful questions that help the coachee get new insights.

As long as that happens for most of the conversation then there are times when it is appropriate to make suggestions, offer feedback or give advice.

Listening skills

Many of us think we are good at listening but in reality we have a long way to go to be able to listen at the level required for effective coaching.

Why does listening matter? So much of the time we focus on getting our opinion across and showing that our view is right. Stephen Covey taught us that effective people seek first to understand the other person and then be understood themselves. This is a great starting point for why listening matters. Listening also helps to build many of the things covered in the bonus chapter on the Core Capabilities of Empowerment. It helps to build trust and rapport. It is a key aspect of being emotionally intelligent and helps to develop empathy and understanding. It also helps to create a safe environment as it shows the other person that they are accepted and respected and also that you are genuinely interested in them.

Finally it enables you to hear beyond the words which only account for 7 percent of what is communicated. If you listen effectively you also pick up what is being conveyed by the tone of voice and the body language. You start to pick up on what is not being said.

Remember – the quality of your listening determines the quality of the other person's thinking.

The next skill of effective coaching is *reflecting back.*

Coaching involves mostly listening with the coach only speaking for 20 percent of the time. The coach's 20 percent is made up of asking questions and reflecting back.

What is involved in reflecting back?

At intervals during the conversation you use some of your 20 percent of air time to reflect back on what you have heard or picked up. This has two purposes: to help the coachee feel understood and to allow them to hear the message they are conveying and correct this if it is not what they intended.

What has neuroscience shown that the brain needs when it is making new connections and getting insights?

Quiet.

Don't be tempted to fill the silence whilst the other person is thinking. Stay silent whilst they process your feedback or question, show that you are interested by staying present and focused on the conversation. Notice what is going on for them during the silence. Listen to their response.

The other aspect of the 20 percent of the coach's air time is **asking powerful questions.** When we say powerful questions we mean questions that get the coachee to think more deeply than they would on their own.

How skilled are you at asking this sort of question?

Open, powerful questions tend to begin with "how?" or "what?". It is good practice to try to start as many questions as possible with those words.

During the course of a coaching conversation you will also use "who?" "when?" and "where?", especially at the beginning when you are getting an understanding of the situation the coachee is talking about and also at the end when they are committing to take action in relation to this.

How do you feel when someone asks you a question beginning with "Why"?

Most people tend to feel as if they are being criticized or accused and this makes them feel defensive. So, it is best to avoid this sort of question when using the coaching style of leadership.

Really powerful questions make people think and can make them feel uncomfortable. Remember, if you don't make them feel uncomfortable you are not helping them to get to new levels of thinking.

Is it ok to give advice? Only when you feel the coachee has got all the insights they are able to get for themselves. You always ask permission before giving these insights and make sure your input is given equal validity to their own input. There are of course occasions when you need to be directive. Again, ask permission first and then go back to being non-directive.

So, the key skills are listening, reflecting back and asking powerful questions.

There are other ways to use a coaching style of leadership. They include handling conflict, having difficult conversations and using brain-friendly ways of giving feedback.

Handling conflict

How comfortable are you with conflict?

Have you ever had a disagreement with a colleague at work? What is your reaction to workplace conflict? Do you avoid it or are you comfortable dealing with it? We all have personal preferences in relation to dealing with conflict. Maybe you are quite comfortable dealing with conflict and wonder what all the fuss is about. Perhaps you avoid conflict as you want people to like you and approve of you. Possibly you avoid conflict as you like to maintain harmony and don't like acrimony. Or maybe you avoid conflict as you see it as too emotional and as a waste of energy. For many of us, dealing with conflict is a skill that we need to develop and it is not something that comes naturally.

Conflict is natural – don't fight it!

Conflict is any situation where your concerns or desires differ from those of another person. It is part of operating as a high-performing team. As teams develop they go through different stages. During the first forming stage everything is harmonious and friendly – this is a good time to agree how the team will handle conflict when it arises.

The second phase that a team goes through is the storming phase when the team approach to handling conflict becomes very useful.

Some teams I have worked with have been made up of people who prefer to avoid conflict. This has kept the team in the forming stage and stopped it moving forward to the performing stage and becoming a high-performing team.

What stage is your team at?

As Patrick Lencioni points out in his Five Dysfunctions of a Team[10], once the team has built a solid foundation of trust it needs to develop its ability to handle conflict.

The role of the leader is, therefore, to bring that conflict to the surface and then to help resolve it.

Why is this ability to manage conflict such an important skill?

Teams are made up of difference and yet they have to work together to achieve their objectives. How effectively do you and your team handle conflict? Too little conflict creates an artificial harmony where there is not enough robust discussion and debate for good decisions to be made. Too much conflict, especially if it becomes personal, can be very destructive. The ideal conflict point is just before it becomes destructive. Teams need to operate in this slightly uncomfortable place so that they can have open dialogue and make the best decisions for the organization.

There are three different types of conflict that can occur in the workplace – relationship conflict, task conflict and process conflict. Relationship conflict is not helpful and needs to be resolved as soon as possible.

What benefits do task and process conflict bring? Handled well, they result in innovation, better decisions and improved performance.

Why do workplace conflicts build?

This comes back to people avoiding having difficult conversations out of fear of conflict. Even the word conflict creates fear. What other words could you use instead of the word conflict? At the end of the day, all this is about is diversity and difference and having the courage to be assertive and speak openly and honestly about the impact of other people's behavior on you. Assertiveness is safe. It is not aggression but speaking the truth about something in an emotionally intelligent way that will be heard and understood by the other person.

What stops people being assertive? The problem is people often take feedback on their behavior personally and go into fight/flight/freeze.

They then react negatively with anger, denial or hurt feelings. So, fearing this reaction, giving feedback is avoided. It is vital to learn to separate the person from the behavior, both when giving and receiving feedback.

Instead of having the conversation when the incident arises people do what Deborah Mackin[11] refers to as "Stamp collecting". This is similar to the emotional bank account concept discussed in the bonus chapter on the Core Capabilities of Empowerment when talking about emotional intelligence and building trust and rapport. When "stamp collecting" someone experiences what they perceive as inappropriate behavior from another person. Rather than be assertive and deal with it directly they open their book of stamps to the page with that person's name on it and stick a stamp in. Then every time the other person does something wrong the stamp collector feels the stamp is validated. Their suppressed resentment leaks out in unhelpful passive-aggressive ways such as procrastination, stubbornness, making sniping comments about the other person or talking about them to other people.

What is the effect of this sort of passive aggressive behavior? Leaders need to help their teams to surface these issues and deal with them. Using language such as stamp collecting or emotional bank account can help with this. How would the ability to surface conflict and difference impact your effectiveness as a leader?

It is no good sweeping conflict under the table and pretending it doesn't exist.

What are the key skills you need as a leader to effectively manage conflict and difference?

You need to be able to model how to give and receive feedback in a way that doesn't create a stress or fight/flight/freeze response in the other person. You need to be able to use a coaching style for having difficult conversations. You need to have techniques to use for resolving conflict between individuals and in the team.

Giving feedback

This is a key element of using a coaching style. I imagine that a lot of you will know about giving and receiving feedback.

What is feedback?

It is information about past behavior, delivered in the present to influence and hopefully improve future behavior.

What are the benefits of feedback?

When done well it has many benefits, mainly to do with improving performance but it can also help people to feel heard and improve relationships.

It helps people when they are learning new skills. It can help people identify a blind spot about a skill/behavior in which they are unconsciously incompetent and move them through to unconsciously competent. Without feedback this would not be possible.

What is the real benefit of feedback? Regular informal feedback keeps a dialogue going about performance throughout the year as opposed to once a year at the annual appraisal and, if done in the right way, this can have a positive impact.

Why do we often avoid giving regular feedback?

The key excuses are a lack of time, fear of getting a negative reaction, which is linked with our need to be liked, and not knowing how to do it. These excuses assume that feedback is going to be negative or, as it is often called, constructive. Indeed, that is the main type of feedback we are focused on giving in organizations. And that is not just in organizations.

Feedback is a gift

Of all the feedback we get in life up to the age of 21, only 6 percent is positive and most of that is given when we have just been born!

Nancy Kline[12], author and creator of *The Thinking Environment approach* which is explained in her *Time to Think* books, recommends a ratio of 5:1 in terms of positive to negative feedback in organizations.

How often do you give positive feedback? How often do you receive it? Many leaders are embarrassed to give positive feedback and their people are often equally as embarrassed to receive it. Neuroscience has shown us that positive feedback and encouragement is 13 times more effective than constructive feedback in helping to create new neural pathways and change behavior. We need to get more used to giving regular positive informal feedback if we want to improve performance.

You often hear people say that even constructive feedback is a gift to help you improve. I remember saying this in a workshop I was delivering in China on giving and receiving feedback as part of a global culture change program. The Chinese were reluctant to give feedback, especially to anyone more senior than themselves, as it was counter cultural. When they started to see why it could be a gift for the other person I couldn't stop them giving feedback!

What would it take for you to make giving feedback and praise an everyday occurrence? What would be the impact if you did so?

What often happens when we receive challenging or difficult feedback?

Many of us have been trained to listen and say thank you.

However, the natural response may well be to see it as a threat and therefore go into fight/flight/freeze.

What sort of reactions have you experienced when giving or receiving difficult feedback?

It is quite normal to initially feel shock, denial and anger. Sometimes this passes quite quickly but other times it lasts for quite a while. Eventually, there will come a point where the feedback is accepted and only then can the person move forward and act on it. There is no point coaching someone who has not reached acceptance.

It is worth explaining this to them and then giving them the time they need to process the feedback.

What I find when clients start to use the coaching style of leadership is that there is a shift in their motivation. Instead of being motivated by personal achievement they become motivated by seeing their people learn and grow and the difference they are making both to those individuals and to the organization as a whole.

Reflection space

How would you rate yourself out of 10 (where 10 is the best score) for using a coaching style of leadership?

Why does it matter that you are effective in using a coaching style of leadership?

Which aspect of using a coaching style do you want to focus on improving to enhance your ability to use this style?

STAGE FIVE – ENGAGEMENT MATTERS

Chapter 11
Engaging the People Who Influence Your Results

"The message is increasingly clear, corporations that effectively serve the needs of all their key stakeholders will outperform their peers. We are entering into a new economic era ... of accelerating stakeholder consciousness and connectivity which will make it an imperative for corporate leaders to master the art of organizational metamorphosis – of transforming their organizations from near-sighted shareholder-centric systems to organizations designed to serve all of their stakeholders all the time. Those organizations that learn to make that shift will survive and thrive. Those that don't won't."

M. Thomas and B. Veltrop, Internal Transformation of Corporations

What is stakeholder engagement?

Mike Clayton, who wrote *The Influence Agenda*[13], did some great research into this. He identified the first use of the word "stakeholder" as being in the early 18th century to describe someone involved in gambling who was the holder of a wager or bet.

With regard to the business use of the word stakeholder this has emerged over the decades; in the late 19th century corporate owners were expected to focus solely on their shareholders but by the 1940s there was talk of managers needing to balance the needs of "multiple communities" by creating secure jobs for employees, making better quality products for customers and looking after the welfare of the community.

By the early 1960s, the concept of stakeholders had been created. In 1963, the Stanford Research Institute coined the phrase stakeholder as a play on the words shareholder and stockholder, and a few years later Igor Ansoff developed his stakeholder theory which stated that companies have various stakeholders, all of which need to get some satisfaction from the actions of the corporation.

By the 1980s stakeholder management was well established as a discipline and since the 1990s use of the word stakeholder in organizations has become commonplace. That is not to say that all organizations follow these principles; there are many who still focus primarily on meeting the needs of their shareholders.

For our purposes it is useful to have two working definitions of stakeholders.

Firstly, at the level of the organization a stakeholder can be defined as anyone who affects or is affected by the organization. This can include employees, suppliers, shareholders, local communities and can even be extended to include the environment.

At the level of a team or an individual leader within the organization, a stakeholder is anyone who has an "interest" in what you are doing, how you are doing it and the outcomes of what you are doing. The word interest can mean that they influence what you are doing or are affected by what you are doing.

With the development of the Triple Bottom Line reporting (People, Planet and Profit) approach, the corporate social responsibility agenda and the growth in the importance of business ethics, meeting the needs of all stakeholders is a requirement of modern organizations if they are to be sustainable.

So, now let's have a look at the word "engagement" and what that means:

When we use the word engagement in personal relationships it is a formal agreement to get married. In the business world, it has similar connotations – it refers to the state of being emotionally involved or committed to something or someone.

So, that leads us to stakeholder engagement. Stakeholder engagement is a relatively recent phenomenon which really emerged as a managerial discipline about 10 years ago. Prior to that, there were two distinct phases. During the first phase organizations and the individuals within them didn't have stakeholder relationships and as such they merely reacted when there was a crisis and tried to manage it. This created hostility and left the organization in a vulnerable position.

In the 1980s and 1990s, as awareness of the need to satisfy various stakeholders started to be understood, stakeholder management developed. This was more proactive and involved regular contact with stakeholders but was very much a defensive approach. It involved making a decision or coming up with a solution, implementing it and then defending it against resistance.

The difference between stakeholder management and stakeholder engagement is that engagement is two-way and more of a win-win approach. It is about involving stakeholders in what you are doing and being prepared to adapt or change as you take their views or needs into account. It is a more collaborative approach and can result in co-creating the way forward.

In some situations, stakeholder engagement is more like a consultation process undertaken by the organization to ensure stakeholder views are taken into account in strategy development or when making key decisions. In other situations, it is very much about developing collaborative, win-win relationships based on mutual understanding through which the parties collaborate to deliver shared outcomes.

Why engage employees?

Employees are a key stakeholder group for all organizations. An important aspect of stakeholder engagement that has received a lot of attention in recent years is employee engagement. Research conducted by David Macleod and Nita Clarke[14] was able to demonstrate the bottom line impact of employee engagement. They did this by gathering evidence from high-profile organizations. Marks and Spencer was able to show that improving engagement had an impact on sales. A large study by Towers Watson was able to show the link between employee engagement and operating income. They determined through their research that 80 percent of the variation in employee engagement sits with the Line Manager.

Do you have direct reports? If so, take the time to develop your own why – why do you need to take the time to effectively engage your direct reports?

What helps to create employee engagement?

The keys to employee engagement are:
- Treating people as individuals and seeking to understand them
- Coaching and appropriately stretching them
- Showing a commitment to their development

In addition, engagement is enhanced when leaders:
- develop a strong strategic narrative or story that employees can buy into
- are role models for the organization's values

Employee engagement is a topic in its own right as is organizational stakeholder engagement. We are going to focus for the rest of this chapter on the sort of stakeholder engagement that a leadership team, individual leader or internal expert would get involved in.

Why is stakeholder engagement important?

Some of the benefits that my clients have experienced are:
- Sharing information and insights ensures better decision making which is key to the success of the organization

- More effective relationships which again results in better decision making
- Learning and growth from creating collective intelligence that is greater than the intelligence available to the separate stakeholders. This collective intelligence can create competitive advantage in the marketplace
- Creating an environment in which individuals can develop skills in dialogue and collaboration to enhance their personal effectiveness and impact

Freda was sitting at her desk feeling rather less frazzled than usual. Her plan for the departmental restructure was finally complete and Tony, the MD, was happy with it. She'd enjoyed pulling her ideas together and crunching the data. The numbers added up and she could see exactly how it would all work. Her next task was to get people on board. The restructure would mean big changes in job roles and team composition, with some posts being moved to different locations, but she was sure that most people would see the logic of the argument.

She knew that a few wouldn't be happy, of course. Ali Taylor, for example. "But that's his problem," Freda thought, "not mine. Ali's never happy with anything and I don't have time to sort out his personality deficiencies right now." A picture of Ali sitting with his regular lunch mates in the canteen came into her head. She dismissed it quickly. Yes, Ali had been at Murray's Medical Molds a long time, and he was influential. But it would be fine. She'd done the research and it was obvious her plan was the right way forward.

Freda hadn't spoken to people much as she was putting the plans together. She wanted to focus on the core facts, finding ways to fit in with the company vision and strategy, linking in with the wider company restructure. She'd seen that Effective Ellie had taken a different approach, holding lots of meetings with her team and bringing ideas to management meetings to talk through. But Freda had felt that wouldn't be helpful. People would only see things from their own personal perspective and too many opinions would, in any case, just muddy the waters. And anyway, she'd known all the more senior people for long enough to have a pretty good idea of what they think.

As Freda opened up PowerPoint to start working on her presentation to the department about the restructure, the phone rang. It was Kim Lee, lab head at the Gutteridge Institute, one of Murray's oldest customers. "I've been speaking to Ali Taylor," Kim said. "He tells me you're restructuring your operations. It would be good to talk to you about what that might mean for us. I'm concerned about disruption to our mold supplies. We just can't afford any glitches."

What was Ali doing, telling customers before he even knew any of the details? "There's no need to be concerned," Freda replied. "The whole idea is that everything will be much more efficient afterwards. We'll arrange a meeting further down the line."

Freda kept the conversation short and put the phone down with relief. She was a little surprised that a customer would be worried at this stage. After all, Murray's had always provided a good service. She'd have expected customers to trust that would continue regardless.

Getting back to her presentation, Freda started to pull the information together into neat bullet point lists to create detailed charts and graphs. She wanted to tell everyone at once; that would be the fairest way. She would explain the arguments and give them the reasons behind her decision. After all, they're scientists; they would go with the facts.

Wouldn't they?

What is the process of stakeholder engagement?

One of the absolute requirements of effective stakeholder engagement is to ensure that you have a process to guide it. I have suggested one here but ideally you will develop your own, one that works for you in your situation.

The first few stages involve doing some stakeholder analytics – this is about identifying your stakeholders, understanding their needs and their expectations, mapping and segmenting them and on the basis of this developing a vision and strategy for your stakeholder engagement.

Once you have done that you need to prepare what you actually need for engaging each of your stakeholder groups. You then implement the engagement strategy and finally you review your progress.

Stakeholder Engagement Process

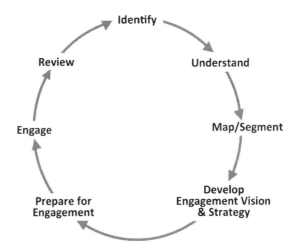

Step One – Identify your stakeholders

It is important to open your perspective in all directions when determining who your stakeholders are. You need to ask yourself who are the people affected by your work, who have an influence over it or have an interest in its successful conclusion.

Step Two – Understand your stakeholders

Understanding your stakeholders is about doing stakeholder analytics. This will undoubtedly involve information gathering. Some of this information may already be available within the organization so it is about doing some digging and collating the information.

For your key stakeholders, however, there is no substitute for having a dialogue with them. You need to really understand them, what their priorities and concerns are, what makes them tick and what their needs and expectations are.

Step Three – Segment your stakeholders

Having taken the time to gather all of this information you need to now reflect on it and do some analysis which helps you to segment your stakeholders. A common approach to stakeholder segmentation is to map them according to their influence or power over the outcomes you are concerned with and their level of interest in them.

Influence/Interest Grid for Stakeholder Segmentation

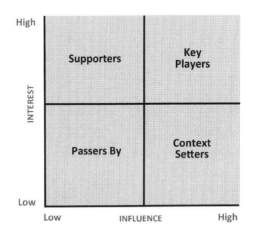

In this example of an interest/influence grid, you can see that you can give labels to different segments of stakeholders. You can then map your stakeholders onto these segments.

Taking the time for stakeholder analytics in this way will ensure that your stakeholder engagement will be carried out with empathy and understanding. This will ensure that you quickly start to build trust and rapport which, as we learnt earlier, is a pre-requisite to a sustainably effective relationship.

Step Four – Develop your engagement vision and strategy

The diagram below shows the possible levels of engagement.

The Stakeholder Engagement Pyramid

At the bottom of the pyramid is a transactional exchange where there is no added value.

The next level might involve one-way communication with the stakeholder informing them of key developments or marketing new products to them. Starting to consult stakeholders and seeking to understand their views helps to build trust and moves you further up the pyramid of engagement.

It is neither desirable nor possible to take engagement with all stakeholders to the top of the pyramid. The top four levels of collaboration, partnering, advising and leading are appropriate for certain stakeholders and not for others.

This takes us back to your stakeholder analytics. Stakeholder mapping can help you determine the most appropriate type of engagement for each stakeholder or stakeholder segment. Partnering is reserved for those with high influence and high interest, consulting is for those with high interest and low influence. Other segments with low interest are informed or involved depending on their level of influence.

Part of your strategy might be to move those with high influence but low interest across to the right by involving them and developing their level of interest.

You can create this sort of map for your stakeholders and determine how far up the pyramid you want to take them.

As you move up the pyramid of engagement the level of added value you provide increases.

Steps Five and Six –Prepare for engagement and engage

Next you prepare whatever you need for implementing your engagement strategy with each stakeholder. This could involve developing a story to engage them with your vision. It could be setting up a one-to-one with them to develop shared objectives. Basically, it involves thinking about each stakeholder and putting in place whatever it is that you will need to implement your engagement strategy with that stakeholder.

You then implement the engagement strategy.

Step Seven – Review

When you review your engagement strategy it is a good idea to involve key stakeholders.

What skills do I need to be effective at engagement?

If you are an expert or specialist offering advice to internal and/or external stakeholders, a pre-requisite is your technical or professional expertise. At the transactional level, this is possibly all that is needed.

To move up the pyramid of engagement requires adding to that expertise by developing your interpersonal and influencing skills. This includes developing your emotional intelligence, your ability to build relationships based on trust and rapport, to flex your leadership style and, in particular, to use a coaching style. All of these skills contribute to effective engagement.

To operate at the top levels of the pyramid of engagement you require the additional capabilities of collaborating and influencing. They are supported by developing a win-win mind-set. Students on my online course learn how to develop each of these abilities.

Developing a win-win mind-set

What is the impact of having a win-win approach?

This is what builds trust to enable you to move up to the higher levels of the engagement pyramid. It starts with you really getting an understanding of the stakeholder's needs and priorities, as we have already said. Based on that understanding your job is to help them be successful and to achieve their goals. You focus on making them look good and on their success rather than on your own. If you do this it will end up as a win-win for everyone concerned in the end.

Why is this so important?

I want to turn to Stephen Covey for the answer.
"I believe the win-win mentality is fundamental not just to business but to all of life's relationships. It's the ticket to entry into a human

being's heart. Without a win-win mentality there is no trust, no confidence, no moving forward together."

In his *The 7 Habits of Highly Effective People*[15] the fourth habit is "Think win-win". He wrote a great book about this habit in 2011 called *The Third Alternative*[16] which sets out a detailed approach to having a win-win mind-set. I recommend it to you all. He was passionate about this as he felt shifting to this sort of mind-set was fundamental to solving all of the world's problems and he put a lot of energy into helping with this in the final years of his life.

In many organisations, I find leaders who have a win-lose mentality.

What is the impact of having a win-lose mentality? It certainly makes people defensive and adversarial. It leads to less than optimal decisions.

How else in your experience does a win-lose mentality limit effectiveness? What I notice is that because most people want to avoid conflict they often end up compromising, which usually means that no-one wins. It is a lose-lose situation.

With respect to engagement, if your stakeholders find that they are losing rather than winning you will soon find that their trust and confidence in you start to dwindle and they no longer want to deal with you. So, in the long-term there are only two possibilities – win-win or lose-lose.

What do we mean by a win-win mindset?

Well, it's not just about being nice to people. It's about seeing that there is a way of operating that means that everyone can succeed. Many leaders have a need to compare themselves with and compete with others. This has a negative impact on their relationships. As Covey says, it turns life into a zero-sum game.

With a win-win approach the foundation is the belief that if we look for solutions that are mutually beneficial we will find that there is more than enough to go round. It is a much more satisfying and enjoyable approach and opens up all sorts of possibilities for us.

What impact would having a win-win mentality have on your stakeholder relationships?

Stephen Covey says that at the very least it means that both parties feel positive and satisfied with the outcome. In his eyes this can be built on by the parties involved until they achieve real synergy. At this point "there is no limit to the value they can create together."

Are you operating from a win-win or a win-lose mentality? Now reflect on the impact of that on your stakeholder relationships.

What is the wider impact on your organization? It is my belief that if more of us operate from a win-win mentality we will contribute to creating a very different type of organization for our children to work in.

Developing your influencing skills

In stakeholder relationships you rarely have the authority to tell people what to do or impose your views on others; hence, the need for *influencing skills.*

What do we mean by influence?

Influence is about having an effect on others. It is something we have and something we do – so it is a noun and a verb. It takes time to develop influence and it is quickly lost. It is one of the most important leadership skills in today's networked and matrixed business world.

When I say the word "influence" what comes to mind for you? I sometimes get negative images of someone who uses their influence to manipulate others. They are trying to get others to do things against their wishes or that disempower them in some way. They start out with the intention of manipulating and taking advantage of others for their own gain. It is important in our context as leaders that our desire to influence is founded on ethical intentions.

What impact does influence have?

When you influence someone you change their behavior. You do this by changing their thinking. So, it is about influencing both hearts and minds.

What is the difference between influence and persuasion? Persuasion is similar to influence but it does not necessarily change behavior. It tends to stop at changing the way someone thinks about something.

The neuroscience of influence

As we have heard in previous chapters, people think they make decisions based on logical and rational thinking but neuroscience has shown us that they make decisions unconsciously based on emotional engagement.

So, if we are to have influence we need to create an unconscious emotional response to whatever we are communicating.

Once the decision is made based on emotion the activity in the brain goes to the cortex to post-rationalize that decision.

The fact that decisions are emotional means that we need to use emotions, empathy and stories if we want to have influence.

How do you influence?

Robert Cialdini is an authority on influence and persuasion. In his book Influence: *The Psychology of Persuasion*[17] he explains in detail about the six rules of influence.

You will undoubtedly have experienced these tactics first-hand.

I was in India in February 2014. I hired a guide one day and visited the Taj Mahal at sunrise. It is probably one of the most beautiful places I have ever seen and I marveled at the intricate design in the marble. The Maharajah built it in memory of one of his wives who died in child birth. I could feel the love that he had poured into this and so was in quite an emotional state when the visit finished. The guide said he would take me somewhere to show me how they made the Taj Mahal and of course I was interested.

For the first five minutes I was introduced to some workers sitting on the floor making things using the same intricate in-laid work as I had seen at the Taj Mahal. I was very impressed.

I was then taken through a door into an Aladdin's cave full of products featuring this type of in-laid work and many other things besides. I was annoyed at my guide for not being open with me about this and tricking me into going. However, he had been fantastic at the Taj

Mahal saving me money on official photographs etc. so I felt I owed it to him to have a look (commitment and consistency).

I had read Cialdini's book and was amazed to see many of his rules of influence being put into practice in this store. It was fascinating to watch and to notice how I responded.

As soon as I was inside they offered me a cup of tea. I knew this would set up reciprocity so I refused. They first took me to a part of the shop where they were selling marble tables with intricate in-laid tops like I had seen in the Taj Mahal. These were large, very expensive items. They offered me a seat and got out the order book to show me that other people from all over the world had purchased them and had them shipped home (social proof).

It really was like an Aladdin's cave and each time I said I didn't want something I was taken to the next section where there was always someone who was an expert in that particular skill to explain how they were made (authority).

Eventually, we had exhausted all parts of the store and I still hadn't bought anything.

My guide was sitting by the door on the way out. Right by the door was a display of very small boxes made of marble with the same in-laid design as used in the Taj Mahal. They couldn't use scarcity on me as I knew that there would be many of these available in tourist shops, but I looked at my guide who had been so good to me and felt that I needed to buy at least something small for his sake (commitment and consistency).

I bought the smallest white marble box I could find. It was a lovely box but not something that I needed, especially as I was moving house soon after returning and had spent weeks getting rid of things that I didn't need!

On returning I gave it to my mother as a gift and she loved it. The gift for me was to see the Cialdini rules of influence in practice and to experience how powerful they are.

Cialdini's six rules of influence that I experienced in India are:

Commitment and consistency

We all have a high emotional need to be consistent with our previous commitments so we act as if whatever we have said or committed to is true. This is especially true if we have made a public commitment.

Reciprocity

This is about giving someone something, which increases their emotional drive to return the favor. It is the most powerful of the six Cialdini rules.

As you saw in my story about India it doesn't have to be something of high value – even an unsolicited cup of tea can have the desired effect!

In order for this to work you need to have built trust and rapport otherwise people will think it is a scam. Your intention in doing this must be in the interests of your stakeholder, otherwise you will jeopardize the long-term relationship.

Social proof

5 percent of people are initiators and will do things first, while 95 percent are imitators who are not comfortable with being first. They like to follow others. Imitators want to feel safe; they don't want to risk making a mistake. Social proof helps them to feel safe.

Liking

There are five ways of creating liking:

a) You can create similarity by using their words, body language, tone of voice etc.
b) You can make appropriate physical contact such as touching someone's arm
c) Physical attractiveness creates liking
d) Giving compliments creates liking as long as they feel you are genuine

e) Being a winner creates liking. People like to be associated with successful people, people they aspire to be like.

Authority

What creates authority? To have authority you need to have credibility. You need to show that you know what you are talking about and have executed it successfully. People then see you as a go-to person in this area.

Once you have built credibility it is important to maintain it by walking your talk.

Scarcity

What do you do when you think there is going to be a shortage of something? You probably stock up on it even though you don't really need it. This is based on the fear of missing out or not having enough of something.

Dr. Cialdini talks about scarcity that occurs naturally and how it can be utilized as a means of persuasion. However, as long as it is with an ethical intention, scarcity can be created by putting a time limit on the availability of something or only making a limited number available.

Why does the principle of scarcity matter in influencing? The reason is that 50 percent of people are indecisive. They like to keep their options open. Even if they want something they won't decide to commit to it without scarcity forcing them to make a decision. The other 50 percent easily make decisions and will go ahead anyway.

The language of influence

Another important tool of influencing is the language that we use.

Using simple language that appeals to all five senses helps the brain to make more connections and makes the information more memorable.

Tell people what you want them to do (using positive language), not what you don't want them to do. The brain doesn't understand "don't" and will want to do what you are telling it not to do.

In the business world we often use complex language and jargon. This is abstract and conceptual language which requires a lot of effort from the brain to understand. Avoid it wherever possible if you want to have a positive influence on your stakeholders as it can make them feel excluded.

If you have to use abstract information, help people to understand it by using metaphors. Metaphors help us get our message across with the least possible resistance as people don't question them in the way they question data. Choose your metaphors wisely – think about the meanings and feelings you want to evoke.

Metaphors allow the receiver to use something they have prior experience of to understand something new or different. Metaphors can be single words, expressions or stories.

A great example of a metaphor is Usain Bolt representing his running ability as an arrow or bolt being released from a bow. As a runner, he is released from his starting blocks and flies like an arrow towards the target of the finishing line.

It is important to remember that it is not all about the words you speak. 55 percent of communication is body language and what you can observe. This means that we cannot not communicate. Even if we are in a room in silence we are still communicating. When we are communicating with another person we consciously pay attention to the 7 percent (words) and the unconscious mind picks up the other 93 percent (body language and tone of voice). If what we are picking up unconsciously doesn't match with the words, we notice that there is incongruence, which causes us not to trust the other person. So, we are unlikely to be influenced by them.

Why is storytelling so effective?

As Arianna Huffington, founder of the Huffington Post, says, people think in stories, not statistics

Stories are brain-friendly. Our brain is designed to recognize patterns so we can quickly predict what is most likely to happen next.

Narrative is an instantly recognizable familiar form. We can relax because we know where we're going. We also know that each story offers something new and different.

Our brain loves both patterns (familiar, comforting) and difference (curiosity, standing out from the crowd).

Storytelling makes people both relaxed and curious, a great combination to maintain concentration and increase the ability to influence and persuade.

Our brain loves novelty so a surprise twist in the story holds our attention longer.

Storytelling is one of the most important skills for being influential as a leader.

So, to make your communication brain-friendly...

- Keep it short and simple
- Appeal to all the senses
- Use positive language
- Avoid jargon
- Use metaphors and stories
- Make sure your words, body language and tone are congruent

Developing your collaboration skills

What is involved in effectively collaborating?

When you ask any business these days what is going to be key to their future success they usually mention collaboration.

Why is this? The context in which businesses operate is fast moving, complex and networked. As a result it is becoming ever more difficult for individual companies or departments within companies to innovate and create the value needed for sustainable success. So, what we are seeing is more collaboration through partnerships, joint ventures, outsourcing etc.

This also applies to leadership – a leader with a great vision can start a business but it takes a collaboration of many people to make it a success. Often many of the people who are critical to the success of the organization don't report to the leader directly and increasingly they aren't even employed by the leader's business. Leaders need to be able to work across organizational boundaries to deliver results. They have to take the time to build relationships and to share control. Stakeholder engagement is a key aspect of this need to collaborate across team and organizational boundaries.

What exactly do we mean by collaboration?

There are many different definitions. It is often confused with innovation, communication and with teamwork.

Having read many of the definitions, I think that this one given by Carlos Dominguez in the Cisco Blog in 2011 is pretty comprehensive:

"Collaboration is highly diversified teams working together inside and outside a company with the purpose to create value by improving innovation, customer relationships and efficiency while leveraging technology for effective interactions in the virtual and physical space."

In their book on collaborative leadership, David Archer and Alex Cameron provide a simpler definition:

"People and organizations succeed in achieving things together that they could not achieve on their own."

So, how does collaboration differ from teamwork?

Sam Silverstein says that "teamwork and collaboration are cousins, but they're not twins."

There are some assumptions that can be made about teamwork – people are aware that they need to work together to achieve a shared goal, they have a team leader and for some of the work team members collaborate and for some of it they work individually.

With collaboration the parties work directly together towards creating shared value and win-win outcomes but they often have competing goals as well.

The collaborative process needs to be flexible and dynamic as often the parties have to work out what a win-win outcome would look like.

Because it takes time to build the high trust required for collaboration it tends to be longer term than teamwork and more strategic. In collaborative relationships there is no team leader.

Collaboration brings out the best in people

I believe that there are three key aspects to collaboration:
* The intention to collaborate
* The collaborative process and collaborative behaviors

- The shared outcome

When I work with leadership teams on their collaboration skills they actually start to experience the benefits of collaborative working. They see that collaboration brings out the best in people and reveals hidden talents!

All of these skills enable you to add value to your stakeholder relationships.

To access the final of the six keys to becoming a great leader, download the bonus chapter on Catalyzing Change in Yourself and Others once you have completed your reflections on this chapter.

You can download the bonus chapter on Catalyzing Change in Yourself and Others here:

https://suecoyne.com/stopdoingstartleading/

Reflection space

Give yourself a score out of 10 (where 10 is the best score) according to how you rate your ability to effectively engage your stakeholders

Why does this matter?

What one step do you want to take to improve your ability to effectively engage your stakeholders

Chapter 12
Your Future – Stop Doing, Start Leading Today

Most of the leaders I come across are task oriented. They spend their time on *what* they are *doing* – implementing the strategy, reaching the targets and delivering on the objectives. They often work in organizations that are relentlessly focused on meeting short-term financial targets in order to keep shareholders and investors happy. This creates high pressure, high stress environments which risk leaders and employees burning out.

Not only is this not sustainable but it is not acceptable in the 21st century. What helps to create sustainable success for organizations is having great leaders who also focus on the *why* and the *how*, who know how to create the conditions in which they themselves thrive so that they can create environments in which their people thrive. All of which results in the organization thriving and brings sustainable success for everyone.

Let's eavesdrop on Freda. She is reflecting in her journal on what has happened over the last 12 months since she started applying the principles that I outline in this book.

Wow what a journey!

I was so frazzled a year ago. What started to change this was developing a new definition of what success means to me. I learnt about Triple H leadership and got in touch with how to create happiness for myself and others, why it is important to create the time to look after myself and my own well-being and how to make time choices that mean that I deliver on my key priorities and have time for rest and recovery.

How different my life looks now. I regularly go dancing with friends and am getting quite good at it. I also have a personal trainer who has helped me with my nutrition as well as putting me through my paces exercise-wise. I bought a watch that shows me how many hours I sleep at night and what the quality of that sleep is. I now calculate what time I go to bed to ensure I get at least seven hours sleep. I can't believe how I used to sabotage myself by working into the early hours of the morning and falling into bed exhausted. I am now looking and feeling pretty good, even if I say so myself!

A year ago I really saw myself as an expert, someone who needed to have all the answers and fix everything for everybody. Developing my authentic leadership brand was quite a journey. I thought about my strengths, passions and even gifts! That was so difficult. I identified what my challenges in life had been and what I had learnt from them. I then started to think about the legacy I wanted to leave. It was so emotional when all of this resulted in me finding my purpose as a leader, the difference I want to make. It turns out that my biggest challenge has been to find myself and stop pleasing others all of the time. That is what I want to help others with through my leadership. Ultimately I want them to be able to be themselves and to enjoy work and be happy. That is now the lens through which I see everything, and that's not just at work. This all helped to boost my confidence in myself as a leader. I also make sure that I nurture that confidence by acknowledging what I do well and getting rid of that inner critic that previously had permanent residence in my head.

I get the importance of building trust and being emotionally intelligent now. I am so much more self-aware and am getting to a place where I can sense how others are feeling too, which is great as I can respond appropriately instead of being lost in my own thoughts and just blurting out whatever comes into my head, oblivious to the impact it has on others.

Deciding to get some coaching has made such a difference to me. The insights it brought me really accelerated my development. It feels great that I can now use the coaching skills I have learnt to do this for other people. I get such a buzz from seeing people come up with new ideas and ways of doing things and the enjoyment that it brings them when they put them into practice and get the results they want.

I trust people more and am willing to let go of many of the things I used to fill my day with, which means I have time to think ahead about how we need to change if we are to continue to be successful. I have time to build relationships with key stakeholders who have an impact on what we want to do. It feels great to see them also being more successful as a result of our collaboration.

I am so much more aware of my feelings these days. I think I was cut off from them before. Not only did I not feel them but I didn't even know how to describe them! It feels as if I am a human being again. So, one year on, how am I feeling? I feel like my life is flowing more, I am definitely growing as a leader and as a person and judging by what others tell me I am glowing as well. All of that makes me feel really contented and yes happy. Yaaay! Bring on the next 12 months!

What I have shared with you in this book represents an evolution from a mechanistic approach to leadership to one that is more human. It is an approach that is more appropriate in the 21st century and will help you to deliver more sustainable performances through not just focusing on the "what" but also the "why" and "how". If you follow through on the insights you get from this book and the bonuses that are available on

https://suecoyne.com/stopdoingstartleading/

I am confident that you will start to grow into the great leader you are capable of becoming.

Here's to your development as a great leader!

I would love to walk alongside you on your leadership journey and support you in any way that I can.

Firstly make sure that you get the valuable bonuses I have prepared for you:

- To help you identify your priorities and focus on what makes you a great leader there is an e-book on *Creating the Time to Lead*
- To guide you in finding out who you are as a leader there is a workbook on *Creating Your Authentic Leadership Brand*
- To support you in effectively empowering your people there is an extra chapter on the *Core Capabilities of Empowerment* that includes building trust and rapport, developing your emotional intelligence and being able to adapt your leadership style
- To ensure you are confident in yourself as a leader and have the right mind-set there is a PDF on *How to Re-wire Limiting Beliefs*
- There is also an extra chapter on *Catalyzing Change in Yourself and Others*, an essential skill for leading in the 21st century

To access these bonuses right now go to: -
https://suecoyne.com/stopdoingstartleading/

If you want to go deeper into the topics covered in this book you can find out about my online program, The Effective Leadership Launcher using the link below: -
www.suecoyneleadershipacademy.com

To discuss one-to-one leadership coaching, leadership team coaching, group workshops or speaking engagements you can get in touch with me on **sue@suecoyne.com**

Notes

[1] Alex Ferguson with Michael Moritz, *Leading* (London: Hodder & Stoughton Ltd., 2015).

[2] Rob Goffee & Gareth Jones, *Why Should Anyone Be Led by You? What It Takes to Be an Authentic Leader* (Boston: Harvard Business Review Press, 2006).

[3] David Whyte, *Three Marriages: Reimagining Work, Self and Relationship* (New York: Penguin Group, 2009).

[4] Marianne Williamson, *A Return to Love: Reflections on the Principles of a Course in Miracles* (New York: Harper Collins, 1992).

[5] Dr. Carol S. Dweck, *Mindset, How You Can Fulfil Your Potential* (London: Constable & Robinson Ltd., 2012).

[6] A.H. Maslow, *"A Theory of Human Motivation"* (Psychological Review, 50 (4) 370-96, 1943).

[7] Mihaly Csikszentmihalyi, *Flow: The Psychology of Optimal Experience* (New York: Harper Modern Classics, 2008).

[8] Arianna Huffington, *Thrive* (New York: Harmony Books International, 2014).

[9] Shawn Achor, *The Happiness Advantage: The Seven Principles of Positive Psychology* (New York: Barnes and Noble, 2010).

[10] Patrick Lencioni, *The Five Dysfunctions of a Team: A Leadership Fable* (San Fransisco: Jossey-Bass, 2002).

[11] Deborah Mackin, *The Team-Building Tool Kit: Tips and Tactics for Effective Workplace Teams* (New York: AMACOM Books, 2007).

[12] Nancy Kline, *Time to Think: Listening to Ignite the Human Mind* (London: Ward Lock, 1999).

[13] Mike Clayton, *The Influence Agenda: A Systematic Approach to Aligning Stakeholders in Times of Change* (London: Palgrave Macmillan, 2014).

[14] David Macleod and Nita Clarke, *Engaging for Success* (BIS, 2009).

[15] Stephen R. Covey, *The Seven Habits of Highly Effective People* (London: Simon & Schuster, 1992).

[16] Stephen R. Covey, *The 3rd Alternative: Solving Life's Most Difficult Problems* (London: Simon & Schuster, 2011).

[17] Robert B. Cialdini, Ph.D., *Influence: The Psychology of Persuasion* (New York: Harper Collins, 2007)

Resources

Books

Buist, Ken. (2006) *Trust Me: Becoming a Trustworthy Adviser.* Cirencester: Management Books Ltd.

Bradberry, Travis and Greaves, Jean. (2009) *Emotional Intelligence 2.0.*

Covey, Stephen, M.R. (2009) *The Speed and Cost of Trust: The One Thing that Changes Everything.* New York: Simon & Schuster.

Downey, Myles. (2014) *Effective Modern Coaching: The Principles and Art of Successful Business Coaching.* London: LID Publishing Ltd.

Goleman, Daniel. (1998) *Working with Emotional Intelligence.* London: Bloomsbury Publishing plc.

Loehr, Jim and Schwartz, Tony. (2003) *The Power of Full Engagement.* New York: The Free Press.

Rock, David and Page, Linda. (2009) *Coaching with the Brain in Mind: Foundations for Practice.* New Jersey: John Wiley & Sons.

Rock, David. *Your Brain at Work.* (2009) New York: Harper Collins.

Stein, Steven & Book, Howard. (2009) *The EQ Edge: Emotional Intelligence and Your Success.* Canada: John Wiley & Sons.

Tamm, James & Luyet, Ronald. (2004) *Radical Collaboration: Five Essentials to Overcome Defensiveness and Build Successful Relationships.* New York: Harper Collins.

Whitmore, John. *Coaching for Performance: GROWing People, Performance and Purpose.* (2002) London: Nicholas Brealey.

Other Resources
Edelman Trust Barometer results
http://www.slideshare.net/EdelmanInsights/2015-edelman-trust-barometer-global-results

Article in Harvard Business Review in which Daniel Goleman talks about style agility
https://hbr.org/2000/03/leadership-that-gets-results

TED Talks
Amy Cuddy. *Your Body Language Shapes Who You Are*
http://www.ted.com/talks/amy_cuddy_your_body_language_shapes_who_you_are?language=en

Simon Sinek. *How Great Leaders Inspire Action*
https://www.ted.com/talks/simon_sinek_how_great_leaders_inspire_action?language=en

Simon Sinek. *Why Good Leaders Make You Feel Safe*
https://www.ted.com/talks/simon_sinek_why_good_leaders_make_you_feel_safe?language=en

Roselinde Torres. *What it takes to be a great leader*
http://www.ted.com/talks/roselinde_torres_what_it_takes_to_be_a
_great_leader?language=en

Julian Treasure. *5 Ways to Listen Better*
http://www.ted.com/talks/julian_treasure_5_ways_to_listen_better
?language=en

Vimeo
John Kotter. *The Difference between Change Management and Change Leadership*
https://vimeo.com/20000373

YouTube
Martin Seligman. *The new era of positive psychology.* TED Talk, 2008.
https://youtu.be/9FBxfd7DL3E

Robin Sharma. *What is Leadership?*
https://youtu.be/f1kYBXNzp-w

Robin Sharma. *10 Things Authentic Leaders Do*
https://youtu.be/PcnR8ixTufk

Seth Godin on *The Difference Between Leadership and Management*
https://youtu.be/Xx2SV2bYSfU

Simon Sinek. *Why Good Leaders Eat Last*
https://youtu.be/ReRcHdeUG9Y

Dr. Ivan Joseph. *The Skill of Self-Confidence*
https://youtu.be/w-HYZv6HzAs

Michael Fenlon. *It Takes Confidence to Instill Confidence*
https://youtu.be/OijWNR0WmxE

True Self-Confidence: Harry Kraemer Leadership Insights
https://youtu.be/CYuEe__bd2U

John C Maxwell. *Good Leaders Ask Great Questions* (very amusing as it is talking with children about leadership)
https://youtu.be/-bl5WWgSb08

Carl Rogers. *Empathy Lecture, Parts one and two*
https://youtu.be/l4DwzSnU6pc

Marshall Goldsmith. *Feedforward: Coaching for Behavioral Change*
https://youtu.be/BlVZiZob37I

Simon Sinek. *Asking the Right Questions: Start with Why*
https://youtu.be/_I-_0cnj_xQ

Apps

https://www.headspace.com/headspace-meditation-app

http://www.lumosity.com/
(brain training app)

LeaderShaper app – short self-assessment on leadership styles and the Emotional Intelligence capabilities that underpin them. Available on android and Apple devices from the store free. Report costs £2.99.

Gratitude

Gratitude is very important to me, so I would like to take this opportunity to appreciate the support and help that I have had from many people in bringing this book to fruition.

First of all, I am grateful to the belief my two precious children have in me. Alex and Millie are no longer children, they are beautiful adults, and it is they who got me started on the book by saying, *"Come on, Mum. You have been saying you will write a book for ages. Get on with it."*

Secondly, I am grateful for the numerous wonderful clients over the last 13 years who have come to me for coaching. You were the inspiration for this book. Over the years, I gathered the content in this book to support you in your growth as leaders. We have grown together and I thank you for that.

This book has been a co-creation. Andy Harrington and his team helped me to organize my content and create an online program, develop my ability to speak publicly about it and market it online. Sophie Bennett has been my book coach, supporting me in actually writing the book. Simon Clements designed the cover and Mollie Burr created the illustrations. Beverley Moore created the Frazzled Freda stories. The Raymond Aaron Group edited, formatted and published the book. Stephanie J. Hale and Ella Gascoigne supported me in marketing the book. Thanks to you all. I couldn't have done it without you!

Finally, I would like to acknowledge you, the reader, for investing in this book and bringing it to life through taking action on the insights it brings you.

If you like this book, please give it a 5-star review on Amazon

Sue Coyne

Made in the USA
Charleston, SC
27 August 2016